AMERICA'S
FAVORITE
FOOD

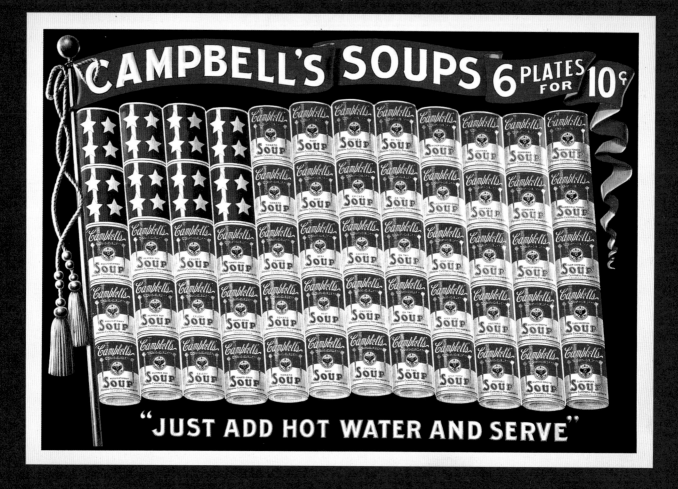

AMERICA'S
FAVORITE
FOOD

The Story of Campbell Soup Company

Historical Text by Douglas Collins

Foreword by Nathalie Dupree

Harry N. Abrams, Inc., Publishers

Editor: Robert Morton
Designer: Beth Crowell, Cheung/Crowell Design
Photo Research: Neil Ryder Hoos

Library of Congress Cataloging-in-Publication Data
Collins, Douglas, 1945-
     America's Favorite Food: the story of Campbell
Soup/by Douglas Collins; foreword by Natalie Dupree.
          p. cm.
     Includes index.
     ISBN 0-8109-1952-4 (trade)
     ISBN 0-8109-2592-3 (Campbell pbk.)
     1. Campbell Soup Company–History. 2. Soup
industry–United States–History. 3. Food industry
and trade–United States–History. 4. Conglomerate
corporations–United States–History.
I. Title.
HD9330.S624C363   1994
338.7'641813'0973 — dc20

Published in 1994 by Harry N. Abrams,
Incorporated, New York

A Times Mirror Company

Printed and bound in Japan

Contents

Foreword by Nathalie Dupree

6

CHAPTER ONE

Mr. Campbell's Company

10

CHAPTER TWO

Dr. Dorrance's Brilliant Idea

30

CHAPTER THREE

A Culinary Accomplishment

58

CHAPTER FOUR

The 21 Kinds

84

CHAPTER FIVE

We Blend the Best

106

CHAPTER SIX

An Era of Growth

132

CHAPTER SEVEN

125 Years of Success

164

PORTFOLIO

Andy Warhol and The Campbell Images

188

Epilogue by Campbell Soup Company

200

Index and Picture Credits

211

Foreword

*As I read this book — Doug Collins's history of the Campbell Soup Company family —
the history of my own family passed before my eyes. My great grandparents were bakers
and grocers in Minnesota and Chicago, and the earliest Campbell products were stocked
on their shelves. My mother's father was a farmer and she remembers her mother serving
Campbell's soup to my Grandfather on a cold Minnesota day before he went back out
into the snow for an afternoon's work on the farm. My grandmother made all the fresh
bread for the farm family twice a week, and soup was the meal on bread baking days,
served with the first loaves fresh from the oven. Later, as a widow, she served soup to her
three children. Campbell's tomato soup and vegetable soup, introduced in the late
1890s, were on her table as they were on the rest of America's!*

*In my family, as in most others, there was homemade soup, and there was
Campbell's. Each was distinctive, and each was recognized as good and serving a
purpose. There was never a time when the women of any of the generations of my family
relied on homemade soup to feed their families. They were busy, strong-minded, hard
working women who didn't have the time to make soup from scratch or who couldn't
always find the ingredients in midwinter.*

*When my father left for Europe to serve as an army officer before the end of World
War II, my mother was left with three small children to raise, one of whom was ill and
in the hospital. My sister and I were cared for by a succession of housekeeper/baby sitters,
who had few cooking talents. We depended on Campbell's soup, and we loved it.*

*While our mother was on her long trek by bus to and from the hospital, visiting
her toddler in a ward that wanted no children visitors, my sister and I spent long hours
reading books. We often prepared our own meals, and soup was a favorite. We would
pull out a small pan and marry the water with the soup, delighting in the change in
consistency and enjoying the rich aroma as the mixture heated. This brought my first
understanding of how sauces thicken and thin and of the need for stirring as they come
to a boil.*

It was a lonely time for my sister and me, and a bowl of hot Campbell's soup,

sliding down our throats and warming us helped us know we were being thought of and

cared for, too. My mother would arrive home worn out and tired and would be equally

grateful for the fast, easy bowl of soup that would refresh her enough to deal with us

and the necessities of life.

Happily, my brother was released from the hospital, but he remained very ill for

some months. My mother was forced to work full time, and my sister and I became his

daily caretakers. We laugh now and say we were the first latch-key children. But, thanks

to Campbell's, we were able to look after ourselves with convenient, nutritious meals.

Everyone in the family continued to check the Campbell's soup shelf to see if their favorite

variety was there.

As a fledgling cook in my high school years, I liked combining Campbell's soup

with other ingredients, making up recipes to feed the whole family. I was a whiz at

making a green bean and mushroom soup casserole topped with canned onion rings.

I still love it, although the canned green beans have been replaced by fresh, and some-

times I might caramelize some onions rather than use the canned variety.

Like Dr. John Dorrance, the guiding genius of Campbell Soup Company, I learned

the need for a good sauce stock in Europe. While studying for my advanced certificate

in culinary arts at the Cordon Bleu Cooking School in London, I became homesick. Off

I trotted to the posh store Harrods — or was it Fortnum and Masons? — and bought

a can of Chicken Noodle Soup. "M'm! M'm! Good!" sang in my head! One day a man

turned to me and said, "Did they copy that can from the artist Andy Warhol or did he

copy it from them?" I laughed and said Campbell's came first. Reading this book you'll

see how and why.

When I returned to the United States from the Cordon Bleu, armed with my English

and French recipes, I faltered. At first I couldn't figure out how to transpose the mea-

sures and ingredients of the recipes. I remember once, having just returned, being desperate to impress some friends of my in-laws while we were staying with them looking for a place to live. I wanted to show off my culinary training — and here I was in a kitchen without even a good knife. I turned to Campbell's, and poured their Cream of Mushroom Soup laced with sherry over chicken and other ingredients to make a Chicken Divan. Everyone was rapturous. I was relieved.

Later, living in Georgia, I started a small restaurant at the Hub, midway between Social Circle and Covington, across from the tri-country cattle auction barn. I grew my own vegetables and fresh herbs, but I couldn't find any place to get beef and veal bones. No butcher would deliver them to me, and the local grocery stores couldn't get them reliably. So back to Campbell's I went, using their Beef Broth and turning out a wonderful Sauce Lyonnaise for my beef roasts.

Much later I conducted an itinerant series of classes in various cities. Sometimes my mother went with me to keep me company as I drove long hours, pots and pans swinging in the rear of my car, like a tinker's wagon of days gone by. We would arrive in the strange city, and friends and students would rush to help us prepare and teach the making of exotic dishes. Puff pastry, brioches, and complicated sauces were our metier. At the end of one particularly exhausting day we returned to the home of a local student helper. It was time to eat supper, to feed ourselves and her son, and then go on our way. Our hostess opened a kitchen cabinet door and pulled out a can of Campbell's soup. Giggling at the contrast between the exotic dishes we'd been making all day and the familiar, we all declared no soup had ever tasted as good. My mother still laughs about it.

So it was like reading about a family member to read this book on Campbell's. Surely you, too, will find it brings up memories of meals you had.

It will come as no surprise to lovers of good food that the basis of good soup is in the combination of first-rate ingredients, their essence extracted through long, slow careful cooking. What will be surprising to readers of this book is just what was required to make the earliest Campbell's soups, for example their chicken soup, the story of which is detailed herein. That story, the remarkable invention of condensed soup that was Dr. John Dorrance's brilliant idea, forms a key part in the history of not only soup-making, but of America's eating habits that are also narrated here. And a fascinating story it is, for it encompasses the story of the growth of a major industry — prepared foods — and it ranges from the great French chef Escoffier across the legions of English and American cooks of the eighteenth and nineteenth centuries. It is the story, as well, of marketing genius and the role that advertising plays in American business. Here is the prescience of Dr. Dorrance and those who followed his leadership in sensing a need for a product before the consumer was even aware of it, creating the product in the best way possible, and then creating a niche for it. The jingles and images created by Campbell over the years are all a part of this, from the introduction of the Campbell Kids in 1904, to the inspired phrase "M'm! M'm! Good!", to the 1994 sponsorship of the Olympic figure skater Nancy Kerrigan.

And here, from an industry pioneer's dedication to culinary excellence and his recognition of the need for affordable, nutritious, and convenient food is the growth of a remarkably successful company whose history spans a century and a quarter.

From the earliest days, the mandate was "People aren't interested in the can, they're interested in what's inside." And no matter how healthy or handy the product was, it had to taste good. Again and again as I read this book, I wondered how the American family — or our economy — would have thrived so well without Campbell's soups or their dedicated developer.

— Nathalie Dupree

CHAPTER ONE

Mr. Campbell's Company

The Delaware River curves sharply around Cooper's Point as it flows between Philadelphia, Pennsylvania, on its west bank and Camden, New Jersey, on its east, separating two cities and two states with a mile of open, slow-moving tidal water. For most of their respective histories, however, about all these two very different municipalities shared was this common river boundary. Despite the fact that in 1688 a ferry had been licensed to carry "man and beast" from one bank to the other, well into the eighteenth century the preponderance of cargo, mostly nonhuman, was floated westward. Cosmopolitan Philadelphia was one of the colonies' leading cities, and sparsely populated Camden was merely a country settlement, a convenient riverside loading dock for the shipment of rural New Jersey's pine

wood, charcoal, pork, green peas, cucumbers, muskmelons, sweet potatoes, and peaches to Philadelphia's busy markets across the river.

Even as late as 1830, when John James Audubon walked the streets of the "little village" to sketch birds, Camden had only a few hundred small, undistinguished-looking houses, many not much more than shacks. Its entire commercial establishment consisted of shops serving the transportation industry: eight smithies, two harness makers, two tanneries, six coach makers. Nine taverns served workers and wayfarers alike. It was a rough town; goats and pigs wandered freely, and on certain street corners local rowdies hung out, "swearing, cursing each other, lying, insulting females, and using indecent and offensive expressions."

The town's favorable location on the Delaware was clearly its most marketable asset, one that belatedly attracted the attention of entrepreneurs from across the river. As one businessman wrote in the late nineteenth century, "Camden is magnificently planted on the side of the finest fresh tidal river in the world, and with a water frontage which, by the expenditure of a moderate sum of money, can be made the equal of any harbor in the country." The broad, flat land along the river was indeed built upon, and the old ferry slip — named, like the point, after its early operator, Jacob Cooper — was by 1900 surrounded by several large, prosperous industrial establishments: Joseph Van Sciver's furniture factory, Hollingshead's chemical plant, the Victor Talking Machine Company, and the New York

Joseph Campbell, Prest.   Arthur Dorrance, V. Prest & Treas.   Albert E. Clark, Secy.

Joseph Campbell
Preserve Co.

Camden, N.J.   Apr   1893

As President of this Compa[ny]
I present for your consideration [our]
first annual report, I shall be brie[f]
and not weary you with many wor[ds]

Some of you will readily reco[ll]
the business when we first took ho[ld]
of it nearly twenty years ago, and
have watched with interest its grow[th]
up to the the present time, and t[o]
me personally it affords great pleasur[e]
to see and know that so many hav[e]
tarried here so long, and by the contribu[tion]
of their brain and muscle, together wi[th]
the combined effort and aid of those [a]
road and in the busy marts of othe[r]
[cities] have each and all so labored as to bri[ng]
about that which we now report, as th[e]
largest amount of business of any perio[d or]
year,

Although the changing of the busi[ness]
was somewhat of an experiment, The result[s]
we trust will prove entirely satisfactory t[o]

Shipbuilding yards. Also on the water-front was a smaller, though ultimately more prosperous firm, the Joseph Campbell Preserve Company.

Since its founding in 1869 this company had undergone several changes in name and ownership and, after Joseph Campbell's retirement in 1893, was being run with moderate success by Arthur Dorrance, a wealthy investor from Bristol, Pennsylvania, ten miles upriver. One summer afternoon in 1897 Dorrance's twenty-four-year-old nephew, John Thompson Dorrance, was out for a sail on the Delaware and stopped by his uncle's plant to stock his shipboard galley with a few of the many canned goods packed by the company.

John Dorrance had just returned home from the University of Göttingen, in Germany, where, after graduating from the Massachusetts Institute of Technology, he had been awarded a doctorate in organic chemistry. While in Europe Dorrance had developed a fondness for Continental cuisine, especially the flavorful soups that were available everywhere. "In stocking my larder," as Dorrance told the story many years later, "I asked my uncle to include a generous supply of soup. What was my amazement, therefore, to learn that, although they put out two hundred varieties of canned goods, soup was not among them."

In fact, at the time there were only two companies in America that successfully manufactured and marketed ready-to-serve canned soups: Franco-American and Huckins. The vast majority of the country's hundreds of small commercial canneries put up commodities such as vegetables, fruits, and meats, along with a few specialty items such as ketchup, vinegar, mincemeat, and various jams. Indeed, in its earliest incarnation, Arthur Dorrance's company, then known as Anderson and Campbell, was primarily a canner of produce, best known for its giant beefsteak tomatoes, each large enough, it was advertised, to fill a single can.

The firm's founder, Abraham Anderson, initially knew very little about the food business. Born in 1834, he had been trained as a tinsmith. Tin, the chemical properties of which adequately resist oxidation, was then being widely used as a roofing material, and after learning how to cut, crimp, and fasten large sheets of the metal, Anderson spent several years in Newark, New Jersey, fabricating and installing roofs. Around 1860, he moved to Philadelphia and turned his tinsmithing skills to the manufacture of a relatively new household product, refrigerators. Anderson was in many ways at the right place with the right trade at the right time. As the United

Opposite: The first annual report of the Joseph Campbell Preserve Company, issued in 1893. Above: Abraham Anderson, whose small 1862 Camden canning factory was in time transformed into the Campbell Soup Company. Below: The Camden, New Jersey, office and canning factory of the Joseph Campbell Preserve Company.

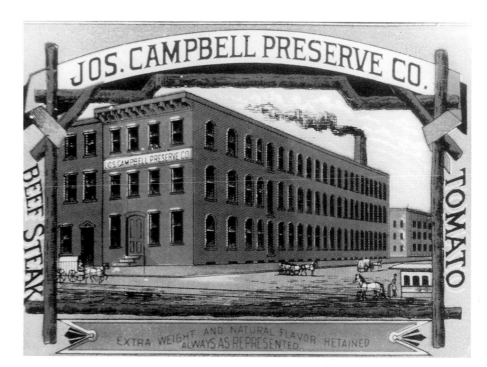

States began its slow shift from an agrarian to an industrial economy, the distribution of meat, fruit, and vegetables inevitably created a demand for new methods to ensure that fresh food remained unspoiled during its journey from the rural farm to the urban table.

Food storage had not always been so pressing a problem. The colonial American diet, though sometimes coarse and badly prepared, at least was varied in kind and copious in quantity. Most food was cooked in an open fireplace, either in a hanging stew pot or in a three-legged iron skillet called a spider. Cooking was a tricky process: a hand over the coals calculated temperature; the transit of the sun across

the sky served as a kitchen timer. But game was plentiful, as were pigs, chickens, fruits, nuts, and vegetables.

The French general comte de Rochambeau describes the table set at George Washington's Mount Vernon as:

English in style, composed of eight or ten main dishes, some of butchers' meat, some of poultry, accompanied by several kinds of vegetables, followed by a second course of pastry, all of which fell under two headings, puddings and pies. After these two courses, the tablecloth was removed, and we were served apples and a great quantity of nuts, of which George Washington ate enormously for two hours, meanwhile proposing toasts and conversing.

Prior to the Civil War meat and poultry were usually consumed within hours after butchering, especially during the very hot American summers that so surprised visitors from Europe. One of these travelers, the British writer William Cobbett, wrote in his diary after hanging a newly butchered lamb in a well to prevent spoilage: "Resolved to have no more fresh meat till cooler weather comes. Those who have a mind to swallow or be swallowed by flies may eat fresh meat for me." Another early-nineteenth-century food and travel writer, Mrs. Harriet Martineau, after being served a plate of meat in rural Tennessee wrote, "The dish from which I ate was, according to some, mutton; to others

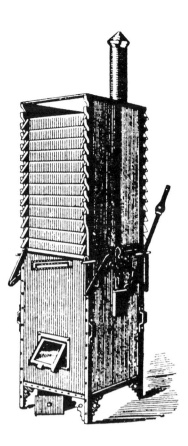

pork. My own idea was that it was dog."

Whether spoiled, badly cooked, or unidentifiable, at least food was easily available. Winter, of course, was a problem, but most American house-wives attempted, however primitively, to put up certain foods for the all-important preserve closet. Fruits, such as apples and peaches, were dried. (These preserves were called apple and peach "leather.") Jams and jellies were jarred and sealed with pieces of paper. (The chemical action of large amounts of sugar on the fruit, rather than the covering, protected these products.) Pickling was also common; beans, onions, cabbage, cherries, walnuts, even oysters were pickled. Though few of these techniques promised much

Above: A metal rack held airtight glass jars for immersion in boiling water. Below: Before the wide availability of preserved food, householders had to shop for fresh ingredients nearly every day. This painting by Charles Markham dates from about 1870 and shows a market in New York City. Humorous in tone rather than merely documentary, the painting (in the collection of The New York Historical Society) is called "Land Sakes, Alive! What Are You Doing, Baby?"

longevity (pickled oysters, for instance, lasted about a week), the rows of jars in the preserve closet, each neatly labeled, were an important part of the family's winter fare.

City dwellers, without the benefit of a backyard barn and garden, were usually not able to take much advantage of any of these methods of preservation. As one commentator noted: "City wage-earners tasted but few perishable luxuries. They were probably better fed than laborers in Europe, but their diet was not comparable to those on the lowest income levels today." Late in the nineteenth century, with the development of better roads and special trains such as the Camden & Amboy "Pea Line" — which picked up the produce of New Jersey farmers for delivery to New York City — many of the problems

with this sort of produce began to be allayed; not so, however, those foodstuffs that, unlike fruits and vegetables, were by chemical composition extremely perishable.

In the nineteenth century fresh meat, fish, butter, and eggs were in many cases not only bad-tasting but dangerous. Abraham Lincoln's mother died of a common disease called "the milk sick." Amelia Simmons, who wrote one of the country's first cookbooks, describes meat arriving at the market "flouncing on a sweaty horse." And bad butter, which the sisters Catherine and Harriet Beecher called "a hobgoblin bewitchment of cream into foul and loathsome poisons," was apparently quite common. As historian Samuel Eliot Morrison wrote, "American cooking of this period was generally bad, and the diet worse."

What was needed for these sorts of perishables was refrigeration. Ice was, of course, the best solution. Harvested mostly in New England, where the long, cold winters produced a substantial crop of dense, thick ice, the ice trade was a thriving business as early as the 1830s. (As a boy, John Thompson Dorrance had worked as a hand aboard schooners traveling between Philadelphia and Bangor, Maine, carrying coal northward and ice southward.) At first ice was a luxury, used mainly by the wealthy to cool drinks or prepare ice cream. By the time of the Civil War a new device called an "icebox," or "refrigerator," was beginning to appear in a small number of American homes. Though mid-nineteenth-century iceboxes were designed in dozens of ways, all used tin in one way or another, either as insulation to contain the melting ice's cool air within the refrigerator's wooden chamber or as rust-free drain pans.

After having been in the refrigerator-fabrication business for several years, Abraham Anderson decided to apply his skills to the manufacture of another food-preservation product that was achieving even greater popularity: the tin can. Like home refrigeration, the preservation of food by boiling it in an airtight vessel was a relatively new notion. Though the microbiology of food spoilage was as yet not scientifically understood, a few rudimentary techniques for the preservation of foodstuffs had been stumbled upon early in history. For most of recorded civilization food was kept from spoiling by the serendipitous discoveries of drying (nuts, grains, and even meats would last through the winter when dried in the sun), salting (meats and vegetables rubbed with salt or soaked in brine would remain edible for months), and freezing (freshly killed game hung outside during the cold months would not spoil). In more scientific terms, if food was chilled, desiccated, or made excessively acidic, it became unfavorable for the growth of spoil-producing microorganisms.

Each of these techniques was common in eighteenth- and nineteenth-century America. Salt meat, usually pork, was indeed so popular that many colonial-era Americans preferred it to fresh meat. (Given the high chances for spoilage, this choice was based as much on good sense as on culinary

Below: Commercial canners used large pressure cookers to sterilize food containers.

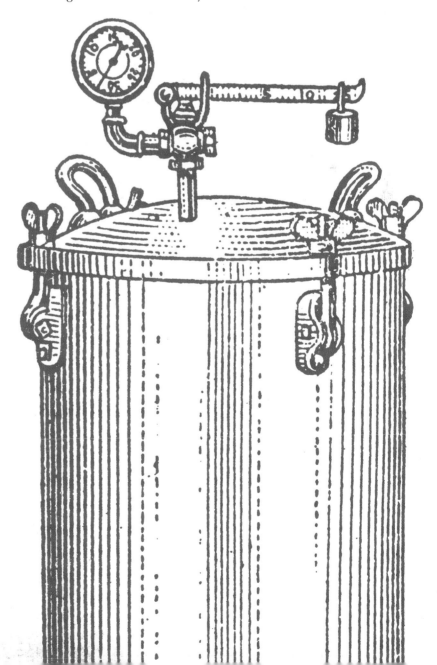

Above: Joseph Campbell, who became partners with Abraham Anderson in 1869 and helped manage the growing firm of Anderson & Campbell.

preference.) As one of James Fenimore Cooper's colonial housewives said, "I hold a family to be in a desperate way when the mother can see the bottom of the pork barrel. Give me the children that's raised on good sound pork afore all the game in the country. Game's good as a relish and so's bread; but pork is the staff of life." Preserved eggs were less common, but according to Mrs. Leslie's cookbook, if covered by a solution of lime and boiling water, greased with mutton fat, and buried in a barrel of bran, eggs could be made to last for several months.

Despite this American preference for briny, strong-tasting fare, in Europe the search for a method of safely and flavorfully preserving food continued. One of the early food technologists was the Italian abbot Lazaro Spallanzani, who, after much experimentation, concluded that everyday air, in all other aspects temperate, safe, and life-giving, somehow promoted spoilage. He theorized that if meat extract was cooked at a high temperature and then sealed inside airtight flasks, it would remain uncontaminated indefinitely. Spallanzani was correct, but after testing his idea and finding the technique successful, he apparently went on to other things.

About thirty years later Napoleon Bonaparte, who was having trouble keeping his armies adequately supplied, offered a prize of twelve thousand francs to anyone who could devise a foolproof method of daily supplying his soldiers with wholesome provisions. This challenge was taken up by a French pickler, wine maker, brewer, distiller, and chef named Nicholas Appert. It took Appert over ten years' work to win the prize, but in 1809 he finally submitted his method to Napoleon and was awarded the money. The following year he published the *Book for All Households, or The Art of Preserving Animal and Vegetable Substances for Many Years*, the first manual outlining the process now known as canning.

Appert described how he filled thick, large-mouthed glass bottles with a variety of edible commodities: eggs, milk, cream, filet of beef, fowl, even mushrooms and truffles. (His largest preserved product, no doubt made for publicity purposes, was an entire sheep.) Leaving an inch or two of unfilled space at the top, he jammed a

Below: Anderson & Campbell
was best known for its celebrated
beefsteak tomatoes, each large
enough, it was said, to fill a
whole can.

cork or stopper in the bottle, taking the "precaution of compressing each cork for three quarters of its length, by means of a vise." He then wrapped his containers in canvas in order to blanket the glass if it broke or exploded. Thus encased, the bottles were lowered into boiling water "for more or less time, according to their nature." Once boiled, that was it. "The following day," he wrote, "or fifteen days after (it is immaterial) the bottles are arranged on laths, like wine, in a temperate and shaded place; if the expectation is to send them a distance, it is necessary to tar them before putting them on the laths."

Appert, now known as "the father of canning," founded a food company, The House of Appert, and the commercial canning industry was born. Canning was such a simple and work-

able response to the demand for unspoiled food that within ten years it began to be practiced commercially in America. In 1817 William Underwood, a London pickler, emigrated to New Orleans, but discovering that he disliked the city, he headed northeastward across the country, on foot. The journey took two years, but by 1821 Underwood had settled in Boston and, taking up Appert's method, was canning plums, quinces, currants, barberries, cranberries, pickles, ketchup, tomatoes, sauces, jellies, and jams for export. (Bostonians apparently believed imported canned goods to be of a higher quality than those produced at home and would not purchase Underwood's products.) One of his labels, on a jar of what seems to be tomato paste, explains his process in simple terms: "This bottle contains

THE CELEBRATED BEEFSTEAK TOMATO.

SEALED BY ANDERSON & CAMPBELL, CAMDEN N.J

the substance of about 2 dozen tomatoes and will keep good any length
of time. It is prepared by straining the
seeds and skins from the tomatoes
and evaporating the watery particles
by slow heat."

Even more important to the
growth of the canning industry in
Europe and America was the invention
by the Englishman Peter Durand of
a lightweight, sturdy container that
could replace the heavy, breakable
glass bottles initially used by food
packers. In 1810 Durand patented a
product he called a "canister." (In
naming his invention, he modified
the Greek work *kanastron*, meaning

"basket," because he thought his
product looked like a British tea
basket.) Durand's canister was a tin-
coated, steel cylinder capped at both
ends by soldered circular lids. In 1818,
Durand introduced his invention to
America, and within a year two New
York City canners were the first to use
this new container to pack salmon,
oysters, and lobsters.

Though tin cans were at first expensive, they were lightweight, unbreak-
able, and easy to ship, and thus perfect
for the commercial packer. By the
beginning of the Civil War all sorts of
food was being canned: California
salmon, Baltimore oysters, Maine lob-

sters, New Jersey peas and corn. One of the problems with this tin can, however, was that its manufacture was labor intensive and demanded highly skilled tinsmiths like Abraham Anderson. At first each can was handmade, one at a time. The body of the can was cut with hand shears from a flat sheet of tin plate. It was then rolled over a wooden form to form a cylinder. A thick ridge of solder, called the "plumb joint," was drawn down to fasten the crimped butt ends of the cylinder together. Next, the two round caps were cut with a tinsmith's circular shears and soldered to the top and bottom of the can body. Food was packed into the can through a hole (usually about 1 1/2 inches in diameter) that had been snipped out of the lid. Once this "hole and cap," "stud hole," or "solder top" can was filled, another piece of tin was soldered over the hole. The can was then ready to be placed in a vat of boiling water and cooked.

Though Anderson had no experience in food preparation, he did know how to work with tin. Perhaps he saw a better future in cans than in iceboxes, but whatever the reason, in 1862 Anderson moved across the river from Philadelphia to Camden and, with four hundred dollars he had saved, opened a canning factory. At first his plant packed mostly poultry, but in 1869 he acquired a partner, Joseph Campbell. Campbell was a farm boy from Cumberland County, New Jersey, who had moved to Philadelphia as a young man and had become a traveling purchasing agent for a local fruit-and-vegetable wholesaler. With his extensive knowledge of produce, he was the perfect partner for Anderson.

Despite the sometimes rather bad reputation of America's eggs, meat, and butter, the abundance and variety of its fruits and vegetables, grown and harvested all over the country, were much valued. The Beecher sisters wrote in 1869:

A traveler can not but be struck with our national plenteousness, on returning from a continental tour, and going directly from the ship to a New York hotel, in the bounteous season of autumn. For months habituated to neat little bits of chop or poultry, garnished with the inevitable cauliflower or potato, which seemed to be the sole

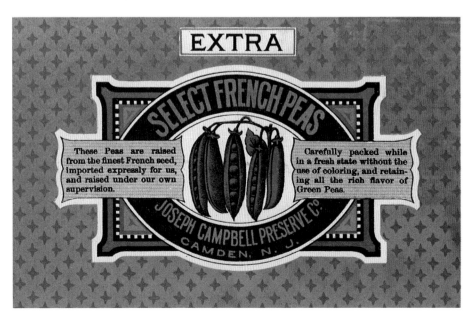

*possibility after the reign of green peas
was over; to sit down all at once to such a
carnival; to such ripe, juicy tomatoes, raw
or cooked; cucumbers in brittle slices; rich
yellow sweet-potatoes; broad lima-beans,
and beans of other and various names;
tempting ears of Indian-corn steaming in
enormous piles; great smoking tureens of
savory succotash, an Indian gift to the table
for which civilization need not blush; sliced
egg-plant in delicate fritters; and marrow-
squashes, of creamy pulp and sweetness; a
rich variety, embarrassing to the appetite,
and perplexing to the choice.*

Given the profuseness of vegetables
in season, it was entirely sensible that
a company such as Anderson and
Campbell would see boundless commercial potential in the delivery of
these commodities out of season.
Though it was best known for its
"Celebrated Beefsteak Tomato,"
Anderson and Campbell also packed
"Strictly Fancy Small Peas," "Fancy
Asparagus," as well as more mundane
vegetables such as corn and sweet
potatoes. Almost all of this produce was
grown on the Camden side of the river,
in the rich soil and favorable climate
of southern New Jersey.

The firm of Anderson and
Campbell, like other American can-

Above: The Campbell factory manufactured a variety of ketchups. Some were sold by small companies under private labels; others, such as the one made from the well-known beefsteak tomatoes, were marketed under the Campbell name.

ners, was prospering, no doubt in part because of the increased interest in canned products that followed the Civil War. Soldiers — especially those on the Northern side, who had the advantage of a large canning industry — found that they did not mind eating food out of cans; it was more flavorful and generally more available than what they could scavenge from the war-torn countryside. In fact, it has been argued that the South's lack of a canning industry, and consequently its

inability to feed its forces well, was one factor that contributed to its defeat. (The frequently dyspeptic General Robert E. Lee lived for much of the war on corn bread and cabbage.)

Union Army soldiers particularly appreciated Gail Borden's condensed milk, a product he had invented after reading of the fate of the starving Donner Party, which had turned to cannibalism when trapped by a High Sierra blizzard. Borden had discovered that after evaporating the water out of milk, "one quart [of condensed milk], by the addition of water, [would] make

2 1/2 quarts" of "Fresh Country Milk." Borden became so taken with the universality of condensed foods that he once said: "I mean to put a potato into a pillbox, a pumpkin into a tablespoon, the biggest sort of watermelon into a sauce. The Turks made acres of roses into attar of roses . . . I intend to make attar of everything." (Though condensed milk made him a fortune, the condensation of all foodstuffs was too large a dream, even for Borden; besides, these concentrated flavor nuggets quite often tasted terrible.)

Perhaps mindful of the success Borden and others were having with processed foods, Anderson and Campbell soon added jams, jellies,

apple butter, and mincemeat to its product line. It is not clear where the two found their recipes or whether they hired a professional chef, but Anderson and Campbell preserves, condiments, and other side dishes did not lack for volume or variety of ingredients. Much like the "rich white soup" recipe given in Eliza Leslie's 1828 *Directions for Cookery*, which called for, among other things, a "pair of large fat fowls" and two pounds of veal, the Anderson and Campbell recipe for chicken soup — which it produced for a time in the 1870s — was a heady stock of meats, vegetables, butter, herbs, and spices: "250 or 300 lbs. chicken, 100 lbs. veal, 90 lbs. rice,

♦♦♦

Below: Canned goods still played a relatively small part in the stock of turn-of-the-century grocers, who offered mostly fresh produce.

12 oz. curry powder, 15 lbs. butter, 1 qt. Worcester[shire] sauce, 20 oz. pepper, 2 oz. red [sic], 16 oz. lemon juice, 20 stalks celery, 50 lbs. onions, 20 lbs. salt, 15 bunches parsley, 5 bunches leeks, gelatin, and 20 oz. celery seed."

Anderson and Campbell products, labeled with the script commonly used by housewives to identify home preserves, were widely acknowledged for both quality and flavor. (The company was awarded a medal for quality at the Centennial Exposition of 1876–77.) That same year, however, the two partners disagreed about the future of the company. Campbell argued that, with all their success, they should begin a process of rapid expansion. Anderson, on the other hand, thought things were just fine as they were and opted for slow and gradual growth. Though the two apparently remained friends, they decided to dissolve the partnership. Anderson asked Campbell to make a

choice: either purchase Anderson's share of the company or sell out to him. Anderson was apparently surprised when Campbell decided to buy, a transaction that awarded Campbell all buildings, equipment, and recipes and left Anderson with skills, experience, and cash but nowhere to use them.

While Campbell prepared the expansion of his business, Anderson began plans to build a new cannery from scratch. By 1881 he and a new partner, William G. Knowles, were once again packing fruits, vegetables, preserves, and jellies. Though the new partnership lasted only four years, the Anderson plant continued in operation, employing thirty full-time workers and close to six hundred part-time people during the June-to-November canning season. Anderson also began marketing various specialty products, such as "Boston Market Mincemeat," then known as the highest grade, and "Genuine Scotch Jams," the recipes

for which were supplied by a cook Anderson had brought over from Scotland.

Though the Anderson Preserve Company remained in business until 1904, Abraham Anderson's relationships with two other well-known industry names are perhaps his most interesting legacy. The first of these men was a Sharpsburg, Pennsylvania, packer of horseradish named H. J. Heinz, who had come to Anderson seeking technical advice and a loan, both of which Anderson offered. After a reasonable wait for the debt to be repaid, Anderson went to talk to Heinz, who, having as yet made little money, suggested that a prized horse be accepted in lieu of cash. Anderson took the horse and returned to Camden. Heinz, of course, went on to become the great competitor of the company that bore the name of Anderson's first partner.

In the meantime, the other now-famous canning name, Anderson's former partner, Joseph Campbell, had, in his effort to provide capital for expansion, acquired three partners: Walter Spackman, his son-in-law; Joseph S. Campbell, his nephew and a friend of Spackman's; and Arthur Dorrance. Dorrance, whose family had been in the country since the late 1600s, was a wealthy timber and flour merchant who, Spackman knew, was looking for a good investment. Once organized, this new company, which was called Joseph Campbell & Company, announced that its goal was "to manufacture and sell all kinds of preserves, jellies, prepared meats, sauces and canned fruits, vegetables and goods of all sorts and descriptions."

The best known of Joseph Campbell's new products was "Beefsteak Ketchup," which took its name

26

from the earlier Anderson and Campbell Beefsteak Tomato. It should be noted, however, that during the nineteenth century the word "ketchup" had a much different connotation than it does today. Originally based on a briny fish sauce called "kechap" used by Malaysian sailors as a condiment, ketchup was, during Campbell's time, a strongly flavored sauce (cinnamon, mace, cloves, black pepper, mustard, and vinegar were among its ingredients) made with a number of different bases: walnut, mushroom, anchovy, lobster, soy, oyster. In America, as in other parts of the world, this product was a kitchen staple. For instance, as early as 1748, Mrs. Harrison's *Housekeeper Pocketbook* advised the British

housewife "to lay in a store of spices, neither should you be without kitchup or mushroom juice."

Another of Campbell's popular products was mincemeat, which he marketed under a number of labels: "No. 1 M. Meat or Campbell Brand," "Mrs. Well's Brand," "Crescent M. Meat," "Extra M. Meat." Campbell's highest-quality mincemeat, No. 1, was probably as rich as the recipe (from *Commercial Canning in New Jersey*), for its manufacture suggests: "7 1/2 boxes suet, 2 1/2 boxes beef, 4 1/2 large bushels apples, 300 lbs. currants, 125 lbs. seedless raisins, 1 1/2 pails lemons, 2 or 2 1/2 N. E. rum (dissolve 1 lb. salisylic in each of two); 375 lbs. sugar, 10 lbs. cinnamon, 1 1/2 lbs. nutmeg,

3 lbs. allspice, 1 lb. cloves, 5 lbs. salt, 14 lbs. citron, and 17 lbs. orange peel."

Clearly, the cooking and canning of such products were extremely labor-intensive processes. Improvements such as pea podders and pea viners, which mechanically separated pod and vine from the pea, helped commodity canners, as did the "Iron Chink," which split, cleaned, and washed Northwest salmon. Manufacturers of prepared foods, however, still set up their plants like large-scale kitchens. Ingredients were washed, cut, cooked, and stirred much as they would have been by a homemaker. The first commercially prepared foods were, no doubt, valued for their convenience, but culinary care, freshness of ingredi-

ents, and flavor were, as they are today, the industrial kitchen's most marketable strengths. ("People aren't interested in the tin can," an industry saying went, "they're interested in what's inside.") In short, no matter how handy, canned prepared food had to taste good; otherwise, the housewife would not serve it.

Despite the customer's indifference to the container, the unavailability of reliable tin cans and slow, sometimes unreliable methods of sterilization were major problems for the industrial canners. Throughout the nineteenth century, however, continual improvements in the theretofore relatively crude canning technologies raised productivity sharply. The first of these advances was the discovery, in about 1860, that adding calcium chloride to the water in the canning vessel raised its boiling temperature from 212 to 240 degrees F. This higher temperature meant that cooking time was vastly reduced, from five or six hours to a half hour, and many canners who had been able to turn out only 2,500 cans a day were then able to turn out close to ten times that number.

Next came the invention of the retort, or commercial pressure-cooking kettle. This apparatus enabled the canner to control his temperature, cut back cooking time, and, since the pressure inside the can could be matched by that pressing on its outside, lessen the possibility that boiling cans would explode. Since the beginning of the industry, canners had been bedeviled not only by exploding cans but also by those occasional bulging cans called "swells," "springers," and "breathers." (Swells, visibly bloated by internal pressure, were caused by leaky joints or inadequate sterilization. Springers, only one end of which bulged, were apparently the consequence of either faulty sealing or a chemical reaction between the contents of the can and the interior metal. Breathers, which leaked, were in reality fairly safe; but since customers could not distinguish them from swells, they too had to be discarded.)

Additionally, the old, slow, painstakingly labor-intensive method of making tin cans entirely by hand was beginning to be modernized. A machine called the "Little Joker" was

invented which replaced the soldering iron with a solder bath in which cans were rotated to seal their joint. (Old-time tinsmiths were furious, and many fought the change with Luddite fervor.) Later in the century the "sanitary," or double-seamed, can replaced even the crimped, mechanically soldered can. The tops and bottoms of these cans, also called "American" cans, were sealed by "a coating of rubber in solution" rather than solder. By the early twentieth century handcrafted cans were completely outmoded, and newer, safer machine-made cans became the norm.

Throughout this period Joseph Campbell & Co. continued to grow. An 1886 history of Camden reported that:

the new company fitted up the manufactory with new and improved appliances for conducting a more extensive business. A large brick building, with a fifty-foot front on Second Street and extending in depth the entire square to Front Street is occupied, in which are different apartments for canning, preserving, storing, packing and shipping. The motive power to drive the necessary machinery is derived from a fifty horsepower engine. Twenty-five hands are constantly employed and during the canning season employment is given to 300 hands.

There were, however, important changes in the ownership and administration of the new company. In January 1892 the *Camden Democrat* reported that "the firm of Joseph Campbell and Company, the well-known canning and preserving firm on Front Street, has filed articles of incorporation since the first of the year and will hereafter be known as the Joseph Campbell Preserving Company." Actually, the newspaper had the firm's name slightly wrong (it was called the Joseph Campbell Preserve Company), and it did not report that there had been a small, but ultimately significant change in upper-level personnel.

A year earlier, in 1891, Walter Spackman, one of the original partners, had died and been replaced by an investor named James Manning. Joseph Campbell remained president, but under the new incorporation Arthur Dorrance took the position of vice president and treasurer. As the company continued to expand, Dorrance managed to acquire a controlling interest in the company, and Campbell, then seventy-six, retired. Campbell continued to take an active interest in the company until his death in 1900, but for all intents and purposes under this new management the company had entered its third important commercial incarnation.

The next few years were sometimes difficult, but having survived the nationwide Panic of 1896, the Joseph

Campbell Preserve Company was in reasonably good shape when it first attracted the attention of Arthur Dorrance's nephew in the summer of 1897. An advertising committee had been established, and a hundred large signs had been erected in Philadelphia, New York, and St. Louis, as well as in other smaller locations along the East Coast. In addition to ketchup, the company's catalogue listed salad dressing, lemon and orange pie filler, Worcester[shire] sauce, chili sauce, preserves, jams, and jellies. But it remained a local and regional cannery, one of thousands. Even more important for its future, it had not as yet, as the young John Thompson Dorrance had discovered, shipped a single can of condensed soup.

Dr. Dorrance's Brilliant Idea

John T. Dorrance was unique among the fraternity of early-twentieth-century industrial magnates in that he was born wealthy and was remarkably well educated. Unlike many famous entrepreneurs of the time — Henry Ford, George Eastman, Thomas Edison, for instance — who climbed from rags to riches, Dorrance's fortune rose from moderate riches to great wealth. His inherited capital, however, had less to do with his success than did intelligence and business acuity. With the first he was able to envision a brand-new product, one that struck the public's fancy, and with the second he was able to promote, market, and manage that product so well that it sold at a furious pace.

The Dorrances were successful brokers in the Pennsylvania timber and flour businesses, and the family could afford to send John to M.I.T. to study chemistry. He was a gifted student, but after being awarded a degree in 1895, he was uncertain about his future. The summer following graduation he and his close friend Arthur Noyes, who would go on to be named president of M.I.T., took a leisurely sail along the coast to the Dorrance home in Bristol, Pennsylvania. On the way the two discussed Dorrance's prospects, Noyes suggesting that, with his intellect and academic abilities, Dorrance ought to pursue a doctorate at the University of Göttingen. Dorrance's father, no doubt imagining a bright academic future for his son, agreed, and within a week John sailed to Europe.

Dorrance did so well at Göttingen that within a year he had earned a Ph.D. and was offered a teaching position in the university's chemistry department. To his father's disappointment, he turned down the invitation along with similar ones from Columbia, Cornell, and Bryn Mawr. The job he did take was much less prestigious, and far less remunerative. Shortly after returning from Europe, Dorrance asked his uncle Arthur to hire him to work for the Joseph Campbell Preserve Company, which Arthur Dorrance did, at a salary of $7.50 per week. Not yet the astute businessman he was to become, John Dorrance was taken aback by the paltriness of the wages.

"As was only natural," he said, "I thought my uncle would pay me at least a reasonable salary for my services. But this taught me the greatest lesson of my life: that when you are either a buyer or a seller you should have a price fixed before you make the contract. But I stuck," Dorrance continued, "for I saw that the opportunity was there, in spite of the fact that when

the books were closed at the end of the fiscal year (I had been there three months) they showed a loss of $60,000."

This, however, would be the company's last unprofitable year, for the opportunity that John Dorrance saw there was not in the vast array of canned fruits and vegetables being produced, but in a relatively new and untried idea: condensed soups. While in Europe Dorrance had been introduced to the Continental custom of eating well-seasoned and flavorful soup with many meals, and he thought that this habit should be established in America.

At the time there were only two major soup-producing companies in the United States, Franco-American and Huckins. Both were selling ready-to-serve soups in bulky half-pint, pint, and quart containers. Canned soup was relatively easy to prepare and pack, but due to its weight, it was expensive to ship. Dorrance had a solution to this last difficulty, one that was on the face of it so simple that it took a man of his creativity to discover it: decrease the weight of an individual soup can by halving the quantity of its heaviest ingredient: the water. Others, of course, had condensed food before this — Gail Borden most notably — by chemically extracting the water. But such a complicated and time-consuming industrial process was not necessary for soup. All one had to do, Dorrance theorized, was add less water in the first place.

He promptly went to work on the problem of manufacturing this product. Dorrance made use of his training in experimental chemistry, a mixing, measuring, and reactive laboratory science that, in its simplest form, is not significantly different from cooking. Indeed, during the nineteenth century a number of European scientists were performing chemical analyses on all sorts of foodstuffs, a fact of which Dorrance was certainly aware. It is likely that he studied the existing scientific literature on the chemical nature of food (*Culinary Chemistry*, for instance, published in England in 1825). It is also probable that he read the French gourmand Jean Antheleme Brillat-Savarin's (1755–1826) *The Physiology of Taste*, one anecdote in which describes a university professor lecturing his cook on the theory and practice of frying foods. ("The phenomena which take place in your laboratory [the kitchen] are nothing other than the execution of the eternal laws of nature," the scientist explains.) It is even possible that he had read the French chemist Jean Antoine Chaptal's lecture "on the etiology of the formation of soup."

In any case, the university-trained chemist John Dorrance was well prepared to devise chemically sound industrial methods for the cooking and canning of condensed soup. What he needed to manufacture was, in essence, a strong stock, one that would hold its flavor even when diluted by water.

Most stocks, whether for soups or sauces, are prepared by liberating flavor from meats, vegetables, and/or fish through long simmering in one liquid or another. Chaptal, for example, in his discussion of soup making, described this chemical reaction in detail, even going so far as to explain why the length of cooking time is even more important than the amount of meat:

This is observed in soups made by cooks who are hurried, or who have not allowed time to pay attention to their work. When, on the contrary, the digestion is made over a slow fire, the principals separate one after the other, in order; the skimming is more

◆◆◆

Above: Dr. Dorrance's handsome home in Cinnaminson, New Jersey, was one reward of his diligent work in the Camden laboratory (seen below in 1905) where he perfected the preparation of condensed soups.

Below: A turn-of-the-century
kitchen, seen before electricity-
powered refrigeration added
another major appliance and
convenience to the decor.

*accurately performed; the aromatic
flavor which is disengaged combines more
intimately, and the soup is of an excellent
flavor. These are the soups of the good
women who perform better with a small
quantity of meat than professional cooks
with their usual prodigality, and in
their case we may say that the appearance
is more valuable than the substance.*

Dorrance's condensed soup stock
had to improve on this procedure; he
would have to load his stock with so
much flavor that it resembled what
really would be considered a sauce.
This fact later led to the use of condensed soups as sauces, of course, but
at the time what Dorrance was after
was a product that was so concentrated
in its taste that the correct dilution
would turn it into a delicious table
soup. Compressing and concentrating
soup stocks was not unheard of at the
time; in France there existed an even

more concentrated soup stock, the
tablette de bouillon, and the American
Eliza Leslie's 1857 cookbook devoted
two pages to the preparation of a jellied
"portable soup" which was "congealed
into hard cakes, resemblingglue."
But these cubelike bouillon products
were neither particularly tasty nor
much in use.

Along with his knowledge of the
chemical nature of cooking, Dorrance
was also aware of the work under way in
Europe on the nutritive value of foods.
The German scientist Karl von Voit, for
instance, had compared the intake of
protein with the outgo of nitrogen and
suggested that to be healthy the average
active human being should consume
118 grams of protein a day. In America
Wilbur O. Atwater had made similar
studies of caloric requirements, arguing
that the typical. American needed to
take in 3,500 calories a day. And with all
this new study and interest in nutrition,
the United States Congress passed a bill
in 1895 authorizing the Secretary of
Agriculture "to investigate and report
upon the nutritive value of the various
articles and commodities used for
human food, with special suggestion
of full, wholesome and edible rations
less wasteful and more economical
than those in common use."

But despite the fact that Dorrance
was well prepared to understand
and evaluate the nutritional value of
food, he also knew that, even with all
of his scientific training, the creation
of a recipe for a good-tasting, marketable, condensed soup was not simply
a matter of balancing formulas and
correcting measurements. "Chemical
analysis is valuable but it only goes so
far," he once wrote.

It may determine the nutritive value, but in the marketing of any successful food product you will notice that these are the prime considerations that have played the most important part in their successes with the public: first, appearance — it must please the eye; second, odor; third, taste or flavor — it must please the palate. You may pack a food product full of vitamins, calories and those necessary units of nutriment, but unless appearance, odor and flavor are right, it will never sell.

He studied cookbooks and sent to Europe for samples of soups. Though Auguste Escoffier's (1846–1935) *Fine Art of French Cuisine* was not published until 1903, Dorrance certainly understood the French chef's first basic principle of cookery: "If one's stock is good, what remains of the work is easy; if, on the other hand, it is bad or merely mediocre, it is quite hopeless to expect anything approaching a satisfactory result."

"When I first started," Dorrance remembered, "they put me into the laboratory. Perhaps I should be more exact. They allowed me to pick out a reasonably inconvenient little spot and furnish my own equipment, which consisted of the laboratory apparatus which I had brought from Germany." Even then, understanding the difference between labor and capital investment, Dorrance wondered, "Just how much of the $7.50 a week I could

attribute to my own labors, and just how much to the use of the equipment I was never quite able to decipher, but it looked as if one or the other of us wasn't worth very much."

Within a year he had come up with five varieties of soup that the company could manufacture: Tomato, Consommé, Vegetable, Chicken, and Oxtail. It is not clear exactly why Dorrance chose these five, but each was quite simple in character: rich, flavorful, but uncomplicated in taste and texture. As such, these soups would probably be most appealing to the American public. At the same time they had that nice blend of sophistication and solid value that Fannie Merritt Farmer (1857–1915), the famous turn-of-the-century cookbook author and culinary expert, described as combining "English thoroughness and French art." They were not exotic or unusual, but neither were they something the average housewife could or would whip up just before dinner.

Having devised commercial methods to produce these five condensed soups, Dorrance was then faced with

two problems: marketing and maintaining quality. The second of these difficulties he attacked by training as a chef.

Three months out of every year I became anything from a vegetable parer to assistant cook in some of the most famous kitchens in the world. The Café de Paris in Paris and Paillards was one of my training fields, the Waldorf in New York City another. It wasn't a pleasant thing to picture, but I gathered my knowledge first hand. From these famous chefs I learned all that I know of the delicate flavoring of soups, and the fact that they made me an honorary member of the Société de Secours Mutuels et de Retraite des

---

Left: A turn-of-the-century grocery store stocked with Campbell products. Below: The original design and color scheme for Campbell's canned soup label. Red and white were chosen as the Campbell condensed soup colors after a company executive was taken with the crisp uniforms of the Cornell University football team.

Cuisiniers de Paris is one of my proudest achievements. This way I learned not only correct flavoring but the tastes of the general public for whom our soups are made. It was while at Paillards that I cooked an order for the Prince of Wales. I knew I was cooking for him, but he didn't. Later in the evening I went into the main restaurant and had my own dinner.

As onerous as he thought his kitchen lessons, the marketing of condensed soups was even more challenging. "We soon found," Dorrance said, "the people of the country had to be educated to eat soups. It seemed to me easier to make them than to sell them." As odd as this observation may sound, at the turn of the century America was not, in fact, a soup-eating country, at least in the way the British, French, or Germans daily consumed soup. America was a meat-and-vegetable nation, a land of huge, hot, belly-filling meals. Mark Twain, for instance, after

months of travel on the European continent, fantasized about arriving home and ordering a large American meal that included all the foods he missed: porterhouse steak; Saratoga potatoes; broiled chicken, American style; hot biscuits, Southern style; hot buckwheat cakes; early-rose potatoes, roasted in ashes; green corn, cut from the ear and served with butter and pepper; Boston bacon and beans.

Soups were, of course, not unknown; dozens of varieties were prepared in different parts of the country: terrapin soup in Maryland, bean soup in Boston, oyster stew in New York. But soup was not a mainstay of the American diet, as it was, for instance, in France, where the stock pot, the *pot au feu*, continually bubbled on the back of the stove. Indeed, some nineteenth-century cookbooks omitted soups altogether, or gave rather general instructions for their preparation. Miss Leslie, for instance, advised,

"Always use soft water for making soup, and be careful to proportion the amount of water to the amount of meat. Somewhat less than a quart to a pound of meat is a good rule for common soups."

What Dorrance was hoping to cultivate in the American public was the habit of treating high-quality, nutritious, and savory soup as an integral part of the daily diet. The Franco-American and Huckins companies had attempted to introduce such a habit, but their soups were high-priced, high-end items, and together the two companies managed to sell only about a million cans a year. Dorrance was looking for a much larger market. He had two problems, however. He first had to induce the public to eat more soup, and second, he had to convince buyers that his inexpensive, condensed soup was, in fact, of high quality. To do this Dorrance himself took to the road.

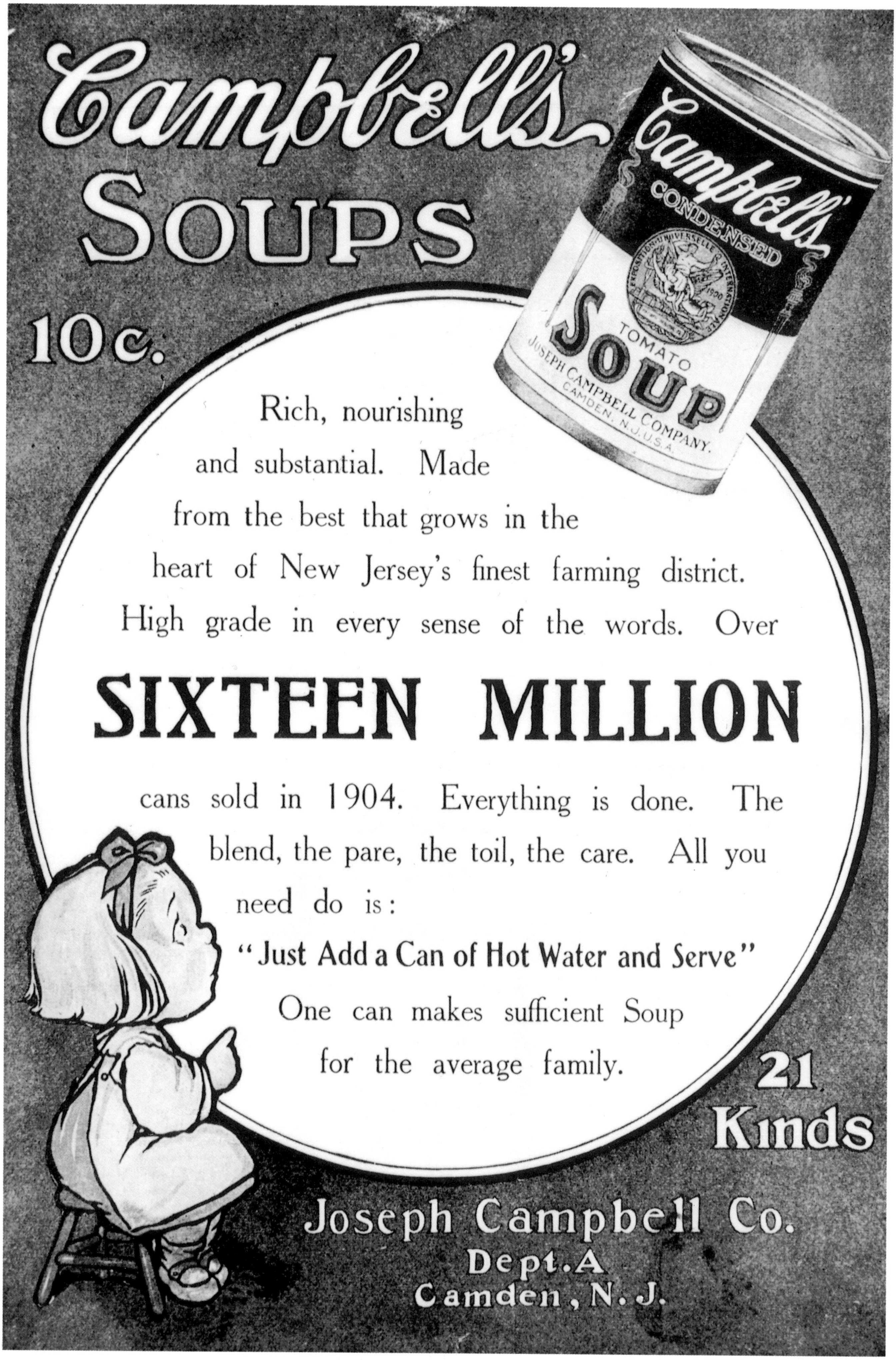
Campbell's
SOUPS
10c.
Campbell's
CONDENSED
TOMATO
SOUP
JOSEPH CAMPBELL COMPANY.
CAMDEN, N.J. U.S.A.
Rich, nourishing and substantial. Made from the best that grows in the heart of New Jersey's finest farming district. High grade in every sense of the words. Over
SIXTEEN MILLION
cans sold in 1904. Everything is done. The blend, the pare, the toil, the care. All you need do is:
"Just Add a Can of Hot Water and Serve"
One can makes sufficient Soup for the average family.
21 Kinds
Joseph Campbell Co.
Dept. A
Camden, N. J.

Left advertisement (tilted)

"A fine and perfect showing. We're gathered fresh to-day. We don't know where we're going— But we're on our way."

HERE'S WHER

Add your
to our advertising

Campbell's
SOUPS

Our big, strong, convincing advertisements
...ines reach and influence **your customers** ar...
...Soups which it will pay you to supp...
...Soups and you'll be rewarded by an...
...h window-dressing material, neat c...
...k to customers whose names you...
and **Campbell's Soups** because of ...
...find them so good, so economica...
...d them ... guarantee **Campbell's Soups** to ...
...reason, return her money

Right advertisement

As easy as offering a cup of tea

And far more wholesome and nourishing.

Wouldn't *your* afternoon guests appreciate a cup of tomato bouillon prepared from

Campbell's Tomato Soup

Try it and see.

Serve it topped with a tablespoonful of stiffly whipped cream. You'll find this combination attractive both to the eye and the taste. Either for an informal occasion or for the most elaborate affair, there could be nothing more acceptable and satisfying.

21 kinds 10c a can

Asparagus	Mock Turtle
Beef	Mulligatawny
Bouillon	Mutton Broth
Celery	Ox Tail
Chicken	Pea
Chicken-Gumbo (Okra)	Pepper Pot
Clam Bouillon	Printanier
Clam Chowder	Tomato
Consommé	Tomato-Okra
Julienne	Vegetable

Vermicelli-Tomato

Campbell's
CONDENSED
21 KINDS
SOUP
JOSEPH CAMPBELL COMPANY
CAMDEN, N.J U.S.A

Campbell's SOUPS

LOOK FOR THE RED-AND-WHITE LABEL

Evidently, it was up to me to take off my coat and get to work. I did. First I manufactured them and then I packed up the white coat of a demonstrator and went out and sold them. Here I met with the somewhat embarrassing experience of decorating grocers' windows in the Back Bay district in Boston, my former college field, and then of standing there demonstrating the soup while interested friends encouraged me by rapping on the windows.

Whether through his hard work or simply because the product was of high quality and compelling, Dorrance's condensed soups were an almost instant success. Housewives who could be induced to try them by roving demonstrators found the soups good tasting, so good that when they were entered into competition at the Paris Exhibition in 1900, they were awarded a gold medal, beating out the more established Franco-American products. Dorrance's soups were also convenient. American households were beginning to make the slow shift from wood- and coal-fueled kitchen stoves to those burning gas, and housewives discovered that heating up a can of soup was quicker and indeed cheaper than the lengthy and fuel-consuming process of making soup from scratch. Then there was the price of the product itself. Once cooks were assured of the quality, ten cents a can was certainly a bargain compared to the thirty-five cents charged by the makers of ready-to-serve soups.

One year after the introduction

Get some
fun
out of life

Here and on the following two pages are examples of Campbell ads aimed at both the consumer and the grocer, whose cooperation in stocking the product was critical to the company's early success. Above: A cartoon image of Charlie Chaplin, looking rather like a Campbell Kid, was enlisted to aid in company promotions.

"21 Kinds"

"Look for the Red and White Label"

With Such a Foundation a Grocer Can Perform Great Feats

1st. The publicity given **Campbell's Soups** is so extensive that everybody knows about them.
2d. The quality brings every customer back for more.
3d. The profit to you (33⅓%) and, profit is the very foundation of your business, is big enough to make it worth your while to help our advertising with your salesmanship, to spread the good word about **Campbell's Soups**.

Joseph Campbell Company : **Camden, New Jersey**

Campbell's CONDENSED SOUPS JOSEPH CAMPBELL COMPANY CAMDEN N.J. U.S.A.

IN WRITING TO

of Dorrance's condensed soups, their sales made the company profitable for the first time in many years. At first his share in these earnings was small. "The second year my services had so increased in value," he wrote, "that I was advanced to $9 a week. The third and fourth year this rose to $12.50 and the fifth year I was allowed not only this increase in salary but also 5% on the profits of soup sold." This "5%" was not an inconsiderable figure; by 1904, out of total sales of just over $900,000, soup accounted for almost $750,000.

Clearly, from his first days at the company John Dorrance had a vision of great future earnings, and he disciplined himself to take advantage of the opportunities the company presented.

After I attained an income of $9 a week I always saved a minimum of 20% of my salary and also all bonuses. This is a practice I have always continued and to this in later years has been added all incomes from investments. Regardless of any wishes or desires I have held to this rule consistently through all the years of my business life and to it I added a promise to myself that for each five years after I was thirty years old I would set for myself the attainment of a fixed amount of capital.

As the company began to grow, Dorrance rose quickly from his initial position of a lowly laboratory technician. In 1900, three years after going to work for his uncle, he was elected a director and vice president. As sales rose, he encouraged his uncle to invest in new equipment, which Arthur

The Maul That Drives the Arrow of Profit to the Bell of Success

WE don't believe we have omitted anything necessary to make **Campbell's Soups** mean success to you as well as to us. Our advertising tells all your customers about them. The quality of **Campbell's Soups** keeps everybody buying them who has tried them and if you will add your salesmanship, there won't be anybody who isn't a regular customer for them—at 33⅓% profit for you.

Joseph Campbell Co.
Camden, N. J.

"21 KINDS"

"Look for the Red and White Label"

"I couldn't keep house without Campbell's Tomato Soup.

"It seems to fit exactly into every kind of menu. And it makes the whole meal taste better and go better.

"You can prepare it in half-a-dozen different ways, and either light or hearty as you choose—a plain tomato-bouillon or a rich cream-of-tomato, or with croutons in it or a little cheese grated over the surface if you like.

"Served in bouillon-cups and topped with whipped cream it makes the prettiest kind of a luncheon-course. Or for a family supper have boiled rice or noodles in it and there is half your supper ready in no time.

"Of course I buy it by the dozen— that's the only way."

21 kinds   10c a can

Campbell's Soups

LOOK FOR THE RED-AND-WHITE LABEL

Campbell's CONDENSED 21 KINDS SOUP
JOSEPH CAMPBELL COMPANY
CAMDEN N.J. U.S.A.

Dorrance did, first allocating six thousand dollars in 1899 and then purchasing an additional plant in 1904. John Dorrance also sat on many of the company's managing committees: repairs, prices, sales, purchasing, and advertising — the last of which ultimately became one of its most important.

At the turn of the century product advertising was still in a relatively early stage of development. Brand names had first appeared in America prior to the Civil War, but most of the products that carried these names were not truly national in scope. Not until the late nineteenth century did advertising agencies first create well-thought-out nationwide selling campaigns. The Philadelphia firm of N. W. Ayer & Son was one of the first of these agencies, and Uneeda Biscuits, a product of the National Biscuit Company, was its most notable success. Ayer helped National Biscuit design an airtight package upon which was printed an easily recognizable and memorable label. He then flooded the country with advertisements: in newspapers, in magazines, on streetcars, and in large illustrations painted on the sides of brick buildings. (Uneeda Biscuit wall paintings were so ubiquitous that many are still faintly visible on the exposed brick walls of older city buildings.)

The Joseph Campbell Preserve Company had traditionally maintained a tight and conservative advertising budget. In 1897 — the year John Dorrance joined the company — its advertisements were pretty much limited to large painted placards promoting its Beefsteak Ketchup. With the initial success of its soup line, however, it was decided tentatively to try out a relatively new form of advertising: cards placed in streetcars.

In a 1905 article published in *Everybody's Magazine*, Leonard Frailey, then secretary of the Joseph Campbell Company, described the thinking that went into this initial investment.

Before a dollar was spent we investigated all the recognized media — paint, bill-boards, street-cars, magazines and newspapers. How much would it cost? That was what we wanted to know, and finally our choice fell upon street-cars, which seemed to be cheaper than all the others. Our first contract called for one-third of the street-cars in New York City for a year. After six months' advertising we had evidence that led us to increase the number of cars to one-half, and at the end of the year we were glad to make a contract for every street-car in New York City. What sort of evidence did we have? Sales! Increased sales, increased demand, and the fact that we were doing only one kind of advertising. At the end of our first year's campaign, when Campbell's Soups were only two years old, our sales in New York City had increased 100 per cent. Other territory was taken on steadily until today we are using street-cars in 372 cities and towns throughout the United States. To fill all the cars for which we now have contracts takes 35,000 cards.

◆◆◆

Right: In 1897, the year of their introduction, Campbell's condensed soups were manufactured at the rate of only ten cases per week, but by 1905, about the time this photograph was made, production had risen to nearly 40,000 every week.

The walls and floors are as clean as your own table linen.

In fact, the need of this is so vital, so apparent, that it is scarcely worth while to mention it.

Reputation.

In regard to this serious point, ask those who have used *Campbell's* SOUPS what they think of them.

You know, of course, that our capital is public estimation.

If this had happened to

"O, I am captain of the Pinafore,
And a right good captain, too;
And ! take one plate and ask for more,
And likewise all the crew."

be indifferent, or worse; in other words, if Campbell's Condensed Soups had not measured to every severe test, we would have been compelled to go into some other business.

But the genuineness of our claims, the searching

For Little, Medium or Large
Here's lots of good for little charge.

AUTOMATIC FILLING AND CAPPING MACHINE

" NO HUMAN HANDS TOUCH THE MATERIALS AFTER THEY HAVE LEFT THE DEPARTMENTS IN WHICH THEY ARE PREPARED."

character of our efforts, the respect we have for our reputation, are all reflected, at any moment, under all circumstances, in any can of

Campbell's SOUPS

If ever it was true of any establishment, we can say that we do not make Campbell's Condensed Soups merely to sell, but to give satisfaction, to provide value, to nourish.

So we call your attention to one eloquent fact, and that is:

During the last five years we have increased our factory space four separate times, and have more than quadrupled our output.

We did not construct an immense building and hustle to fill it with business, but we built an immense business and hustled to get accommodations for it.

Little by little we have grown.

Every inch of space we control we have use for.

These first car cards included a jingle promoting soup and a large illustration of a red-and-white can of Campbell's Soup. Though Campbell's advertising committee may not have known it at the time, the design of this can would prove to be the single most successful promotional decision it ever made. When condensed soup was first introduced, several can designs and color combinations were tried, but none was considered quite right. (Black-and-white seemed too subdued and orange-and-black too somber.) While can design was being mulled over, the company's treasurer, Heberton Williams, attended a Pennsylvania-Cornell football game and was very taken with the crisp red-and-white uniforms worn by the latter team. Arriving at work the following Monday, he suggested these colors for the new label. A design was executed, and within a year car cards carried the slogan, "Campbell's Soups, Look for the Red and White Label."

By 1901— four years after John Dorrance had set up his first small soup laboratory — the company's annual report, taking stock of the previous year's $580,000 in sales and recognizing the fact that the Campbell brand was now nationally recognized, announced "we have gained prestige." Indeed it had. It is impossible, even in retrospect, to ascertain why some products catch on while others, equally promising, fail, but it is clear that all

Above: A Campbell booklet of early date focused on the cleanliness of the soup-making process as well as the quality of the ingredients.

of Dorrance's business decisions matched with splendid fortuity a market demand that he both created and encouraged. Like other extremely successful new products of the time, such as the Kodak camera, once Campbell's condensed soups began to roll off the production line and appear in stores, they quickly achieved brand prestige and loyalty. What had begun as a ten-case-per-week factory output had, by 1905, multiplied to an amazing twenty million cans a year.

This national reputation and recognition was further enhanced by the introduction of the second most successful advertising image in the company's history. As Dorrance explained, "Mr. Charles Snyder, who had been writing the car card jingles since 1899, recommended that we adopt some figure for our advertising." Theodore Wiederseim, who worked at the Ketterlineus Lithographic Manufacturing Company in Philadelphia, and who was at the time attempting to solicit car-card business from Campbell, heard of this idea and asked his wife, Grace, a free-lance illustrator of children's books and comic strips, to draw some figures for the portfolio of advertising layouts he was preparing.

Grace Wiederseim was the daughter of a Philadelphia art publisher and had been sketching little round-faced children since she was a young child. She had been a staff artist for the *Philadelphia Press and Evening Journal*, where she originated the "Bobby Blake and Dolly Drake" comic strip, and she had illustrated the Mother Goose rhymes published weekly in *The Associated Sunday Magazines*. The faces of these children,

as she later explained, were modeled after her own image.

I was my own model because I began young. I was much interested in my looks. I knew I was funny. I used to look in the mirror, and then, with a pencil in my round, chubby fingers, I would sketch my image as I remembered it. My playmates were always delighted with the results — and they recognized me. They, too, thought I looked funny. And I kept on making round roly-polys, consulting the mirror from time to time. Eventually I had created a type that was as much a part of me as myself. And it grew with me, though it never grew up. When I thought of a career, I found I had one in just keeping alive these youngsters I had created in and from my own childhood.

Opposite: A child poses with one of the first Campbell Kid dolls. Above: Grace Gebbie Drayton in her home with others of her drawings of children. Below: Campbell's Soup advertising placards, millions of which were prominently placed in streetcars in over three hundred of the nation's largest cities.

Among the dozens of children's drawings of the period, Wiederseim's children, which were almost immediately dubbed "The Campbell Kids," were hugely popular. Chubby legged, with no necks, large, widely separated eyes, and small H-shaped mouths, the Kids were first dressed as little boys and girls and were posed playing children's games. Within time, however, they began to appear performing adult tasks: climbing a fireman's ladder, delivering ice, directing an orchestra, carrying a basket of tomatoes as "the Campbell's farmer-man."

The Kids first appeared in the newly designed streetcar cards, each of which featured a verse at the top, a red-and-white can on the right, and a Kid on the left. At the bottom of the card were such as phrases "6 plates 10c" and "Just add hot water and serve." The first Campbell Kids car card used pretty much the same advertising jingles as had appeared on earlier cards. These verses promoted the basic Campbell philosophy of

Quality:

We blend the best with careful pains
In skillful combination
And every single can contains
Our business reputation.

convenience:

Mother could make it if she knew
Just why, and when, and what to do.

and taste:

A diller, a dollar, a ten o'clock scholar,
*   Why do you come so late?*
'Cause when I ate my Campbell's Soup,
*   I stopped to lick my plate.*

But we save toil and worry, too.

As time went on, however, the assumption that these bits of verse were being spoken by the Kids themselves was taken into account, and many of the jingles mixed adult sophistication, the Campbell message, and the innocence of a child into one seamless mix. For instance, a boy playing a drum was shown saying:

To put the sparkle in your toes
The rhythm in your feet
I'm telling you that Campbell's Soup
Is just the thing to eat.

Similarly, a little girl speaking on a telephone delivered this rhyme:

Goodness gracious
Oh my, yes
Campbell's Soups
Are grand, no less!

The Campbell Kids almost immediately struck the fancy of the buying public,

and soon after their introduction they were used on all the company's advertising. The Kids were so popular, in fact, that their image appeared on souvenir postcards — a million of which were printed — place cards, bridge tallies, and lapel buttons (which read, "I am a Campbell Kid"). The Kids were also used in store-window displays and in booklets such as "Fun and Rhymes for Hungry Times," which used Mother Goose verses to extoll the virtues of Campbell's Ketchup. The Campbell Kids were first offered as dolls in 1910. Licensed by Campbell and manufactured by the well-known E. I. Horsman Company, the dolls featured composition "Can't break 'Em" heads and proved extremely popular.

It is not exactly clear why these particular characters, among dozens of others that appeared during the time, were so hugely appealing. Certainly with their puffed cheeks and plump

bodies they were pictures of health, vitality, and good nature. But even that does not explain the affection people felt for them. Perhaps the artist herself had the explanation. Years later, after she had been divorced from Wiederseim and remarried, Grace Gebbie Drayton said of her "funny babies":

My children possess all the wisdom adults
lose. With children as my medium I can
be as sardonic or as ironic about things
as I please and no one minds. Children get
away with murder and so do I, the artist
who gets the message across with them.

Though always careful with its dollar, during the decade after the introduction of condensed soups Campbell's advertising budget increased dramatically — from $20,000 in 1899 to nearly $200,000 in 1910. This increase was driven by the company's first entry into newspaper and magazine advertising.

Opposite: A car card from one of the early campaigns. Right and below: Grocery store window layouts, as designed by Campbell and reproduced in pocket guides carried by all of its traveling salesmen.

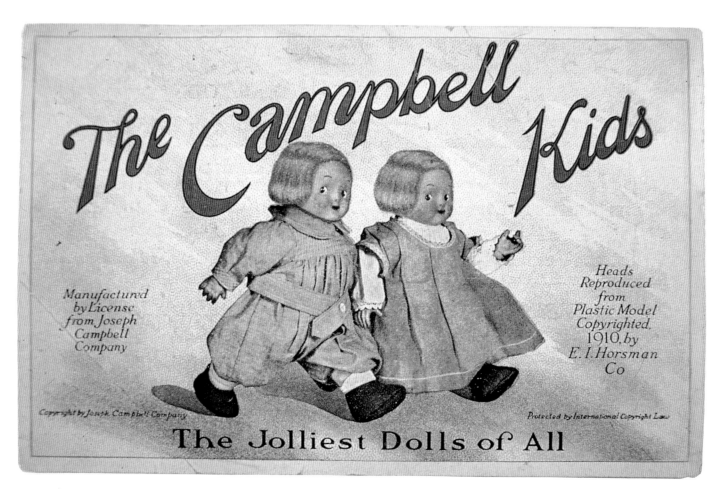

Above, below, and opposite:

Campbell Kid dolls were manu-

factured by E. I. Horsman,

beginning in 1910.

Though newspaper ads were soon dropped as being too expensive, for a few years the company matched its message to each of the available media. As Frailey explained: "In car cards we concentrate on the Kids; in newspapers the Kids and the can; in magazines mainly the can but without losing sight entirely of the Kids. The Kids are almost able to look after themselves."

As popular and effective as the Kids were, however, they alone could not carry Campbell's entire advertising message. Industrially prepared condensed soups were new on grocers' shelves, and no matter how cute and whimsical the Kids and their accompanying jingles were, the discriminating housewife had to be convinced of their convenience and high quality. Their reasonable cost was the third factor in the oft-repeated sale pitch. In 1905 Campbell published a small booklet titled "Just As Easy." As usual, the Kids were prominently displayed on almost every page. In addition, however, there were pictures of factory operations: barges of tomatoes being unloaded, lines of broth kettles, filling and capping machines. These sorts of illustrations were meant to supplement the simple message of the text:

One ten-cent can makes enough soup for the average family. They are made of all the very best ingredients we can get, by the best skill that we can employ. Their use means true economy, for each can contains a condensation. They can be made ready instantly in any emergency. They do for you, at the cost of a dime, what you would find it difficult to accomplish at an outlay of four or five times the money at home. They save the ordeal of toil, boil, pare, blend, fret and

heat. They are all that is superb, because it is as vital for us to make them as it is for you to have them that way. They save you the nuisance of marketing. They make you, to a large extent, independent of carelessness in the kitchen. They are prepared under the most scrupulous sanitary conditions. And lastly — we put out every can under our own label, with the confidence and knowledge of the conditions under which it was filled, absolutely certain that it will be its own recommendation and develop in you that wholesome habit — the use of Campbell's Soups.

As soup sales increased, so inversely were the sales of other products affected, and by 1905 the corporate name of the company was changed to reflect this shift. The old Joseph Campbell Preserve Company, which had been incorporated in 1892, was now called the Joseph Campbell Company. "This change," it was recorded, "is deemed necessary from the fact that, at the present time, the said 'Joseph Campbell Preserve Co.' is a misnomer in view of its having ceased the manufacture of preserves, jellies, jams and fruit butter." Two years later, in a similar move, the board resolved that "during the current year's business, the company will not pack any goods under other brands than its own with the exception of mincemeat," the production of which would be discontinued later that year.

This consolidation of the company's efforts was clearly meant to allow the Joseph Campbell Company to focus on the manufacture and marketing of its best-selling and most profitable product: condensed soups. As John Dorrance said:

When we first began to put our soups on the market we had this long list of preserves which were really a drag on our production. We began to eliminate them a few at a time, dropping the weakest of the sisters each year until we had done away with them altogether. This permitted concentration on a few lines, which made it possible to materially reduce production costs.

This downsizing of the product line was so successful that by 1913 out of a total sales of $6,700,000 only $487 were the result of what the company called "miscellaneous sales."

There was, however, one important exception to this trend. In soup-making parlance there are two main ingredients in each variety of soup: the stock and the garnish. The garnish is all those ingredients — meat, vegetables, butter — that are added to the soup and give it its name (the vegetables, for instance, in vegetable soup). The "stock" is the highly flavored liquid to which the garnish is added. In most cases, however, stock must be slowly and painstakingly cooked before mixing it with the garnish.

This fact created an unavoidable manufacturing problem. If stocks were cooked, as they were, on Monday, the first day of the work week, then there would be very little for most of the workers to do. John Dorrance decided that rather than run the factory on Sunday, a veritable impossibility, he would add a new product, pork and beans, which could be manufactured on Monday while the week's stock simmered away.

Sweetened pork and beans is one of the oldest American dishes, having been introduced to New England colonists by the Indians, who pit-cooked the beans with maple syrup and bear fat. Pork and beans was so popular, in fact, that within a few years of its addition to the Campbell line, it constituted almost a third of the com-

♦♦♦

Below: The Joseph Campbell Company factory in 1912.
Opposite: Delivery trucks drawn by Campbell's Percherons lined up outside of the Camden plant.

pany's total sales. In 1914, for instance, soup sales totaled $5,738,200 with beans sales $2,283,036.

Through these first years of phenomenal growth John Dorrance steadily rose in responsibility and influence. He was the one man, after all, who had contributed most to the success of the company. With his soup earnings he yearly purchased Campbell stock, and in 1910 he became general manager of the company, having, in effect, the first and last word in all matters of policy. John Dorrance's uncle

Arthur was still the majority stockholder and chairman of the board, but he was aging. In 1915 he decided to end active involvement with the company. Arthur Dorrance recognized that his nephew was his logical successor and offered to sell John his interest.

A New York accounting firm, Gunn Richards and Co., was hired to appraise the value of the company. Since tentative plans were underway to move the Camden plant to a new site down the Delaware River in Gloucester County, New Jersey, what machinery could be

moved was included in the price of the company, but the land and buildings were valued either as scrap or by the price they would fetch at public auction. It was further agreed that since the good will of the company was the product of both Arthur and John Dorrance, its part of the selling price would be reduced by a third.

An agreement was reached. John Dorrance paid his uncle $755,720 in cash and 112 notes, each in the amount of $25,000 — and on April 23, 1915, less than twenty years after he went to work as a $7.50-a-week laboratory technician, he became sole owner of the Joseph Campbell Company.

Housekeepers can rest if—

If they take advantage of such labor-savers as Campbell's Beans. This summer, take every possible moment away from household cares and give it to relaxation. Although Campbell's cost you no trouble whatever, they are as tempting and delicious as they are nourishing. Slow-cooked; thoroughly digestible. Serve hot or cold. Order them by the case for convenience.

15c a Can

Campbell's BEANS

Opposite, above, and below: Dr. Dorrance extended the company's product range to solve a soup manufacturing problem. Pork & Beans, however, soon became a profitable sideline.

Campbell's PORK AND BEANS
JOSEPH CAMPBELL COMPANY
CAMDEN·N·J·U·S·A·

Order by the case for summer

Then you have them ready at an instant's notice to give you a delicious dish, hot or cold, made doubly tempting by Campbell's famous tomato sauce. For the picnic, for the outing, the motor or boating trip or for regular use on the home table, the quality and convenience of Campbell's Beans make them an ideal summer food.

15c a Can
Except west of Mississippi River and in Canada

Campbell's BEANS
LOOK FOR THE RED-AND-WHITE LABEL

A Culinary Accomplishment

According to popular culinary lore, soup is one of the oldest prepared dishes. As soon as primitive man discovered the benefits of cooked foods, it is said, meats and vegetables were tossed into a crude vessel, filled with water, boiled, and then eaten along with the flavorful pot liquid. The simplicity of this cooking technique, it is further argued, makes soup one of the earliest meals that was good tasting, easy to prepare, and economical. No doubt this is true; it is just as easy to imagine the fortuitous discovery that simmering food in hot water creates a savory, appetizing concoction as it is to accept Charles Lamb's tale of a careless farm boy preparing the first roast pig by accidentally burning down the barn.

There are other food historians, however, who do not consider the rudimentary technique of boiling meat and vegetables worthy of being considered soup making. Auguste Escoffier, perhaps the best-known French chef and critic, was rather dismissive of this version of the lineage of soup. "The nutritious liquids now under the names of Soups are of comparatively recent origin," he argued, dating them back only to the "early years of the nineteenth century." Before that, Escoffier stated, soup broth was inconsequential and unimportant, either just the medium in which foods were cooked or part of a complete dish that more resembled a thick stew than a soup. Probably there is some truth in each of these arguments.

Certainly, soups of one sort or another have been with us for thousands of years. Spartan soldiers subsisted almost solely on a foul-smelling concoction of water, vinegar, salt, and boiled pork called the "black broth" — which, a wag once speculated, was reason enough for the Spartans being "fearless of death in battle [since] anyone in his senses would rather undergo the pains of dissolution than continue to exist on such execrable food." For the most part, however, ancient cultures had very little interest in broths. Those who, like the rich and cultivated Romans, had abundant quantities of food readily available spent most of their time gorging themselves on huge meals of meat, fish, and fowl, all of which they washed down with sweetened Valerian wine. Sipping soup from a spoon would have reduced the Romans' urge to satiate themselves.

During the Middle Ages and the Renaissance soup seems to have more resembled a heavy porridge than a

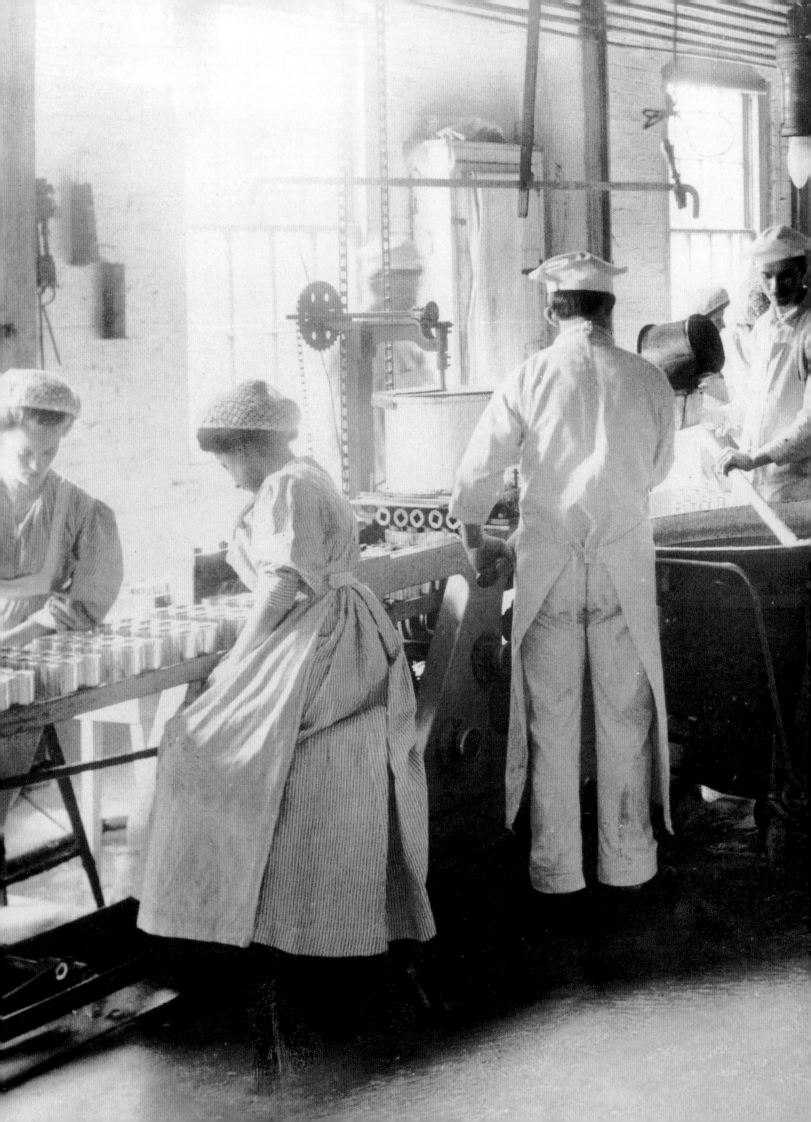

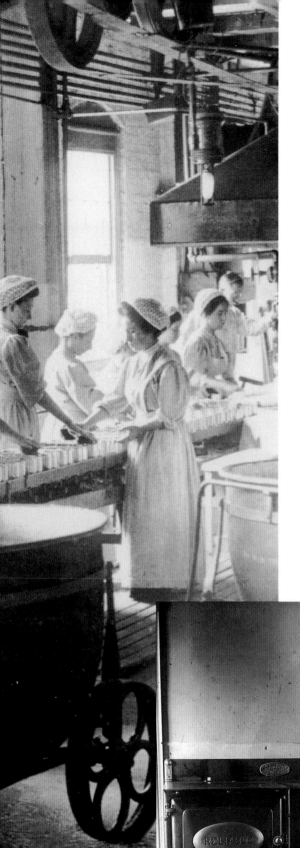

flavorful broth. According to food historian Waverly Root, when Rabelais referred to *soupe*, he meant a piece of bread that had been boiled in a liquid that had the consistency of oatmeal. The English word *sop*, meaning to soak up, Root contends, is the direct descendant of the original meaning of the French *soupe*. At some point, however, the word came to signify meat boiling in a pot. And eventually, French cooks, who had previously thrown away the pot liquor, discovered that the cooking medium was as delicious as the food cooked in it, and the word "soup" came to have its present connotation: a liquid food prepared by boiling one or more ingredients to extract their flavor. (Dr. Samuel Johnson's definition of soup in his famous eighteenth-century dictionary as a "strong decoction of flesh for the table" seems to back up this etymology, but then

Johnson had no particular love of the French anyway.)

According to Root, soup may also be responsible for the word "restaurant." In the age of Louis XV sumptuary laws made it illegal to sell individual servings of meat to be consumed on the premises where they were prepared. The authorities, however, had not thought to include the cooking broth, the bouillon, in their proscription. This gave a meat merchant named Boulanger an idea. He began advertising his bouillon as "restaurants," or "takeouts." He put up a sign that read, "Boulanger debite des restaurants divins" ("Boulanger puts up divine takeout"). Within time the laws were relaxed and Boulanger's soup kitchen became a full-service restaurant.

Soups were prepared in America as early as the seventeenth century. Indeed, some of the best-known indigenous American dishes were soups. Pilgrim colonists learned from local Indians how to prepare a sort of chowder with the abundantly available New England clams. And the explorer John Bartram describes an Iroquois "repast" that "consisted of three great

◆◆◆

Opposite and left: Well into the twentieth century the laborious and meticulous preparation of food by hand at home was echoed in the Campbell factory. At far left Campbell workers fill cans of soup on an early version of an assembly line.

To be the ice-man
Is my lot,
But give me Campbell's
Piping-hot!

RECIPES

CREAM OF MUSHROOM GRAVY

Add to the drippings of a roast of beef, one-half cupful of water, and scrape the brown from the sides of pan. Add one can of Campbell's Cream of Mushroom Soup and stir until well blended and smooth. Bring to a boil and serve piping hot. It may be made thinner, if desired, by adding more water.

This makes an excellent gravy for roast beef and is far superior to the usual brown gravy.

CHICKEN AND CREAM OF MUSHROOM SOUP

Blend one can of Campbell's Chicken with Rice Soup with one can of Campbell's Cream of Mushroom Soup. Add one can of water, using the soup can for a measure. Heat, but do not boil.

MUSHROOM SAUCE

Heat contents of one can of Campbell's Cream of Mushroom Soup in double boiler, stirring until smooth. For a thick sauce serve just as it is. For a sauce of medium thickness stir in from one-third to one-half cups of milk or water. Serve very hot. Delicious on steaks or chops. May also be used as a supper dish by re-heating one to one and one-half cups diced cold meat, flaked fish or hard-boiled egg in the sauce and serving on hot toast, in cream puff or patty shells or between split, hot buttered biscuits. Drained canned peas or finely cut celery may be added.

As early as 1905 Campbell encouraged the use of its condensed soups as a basis for sauces, gravies, and combination soups by producing cookbooks with appetizing recipes. This booklet, designed in the form of a soup can, dates from 1934.

CAMPBELL'S KIDS

Campbell's SOUPS 10¢ a Can
ADD ZEST TO APPETITE

kettles of Indian corn soup, or thin hominy, with dried eels and other fish boiled in it and one kettle full of young squashes and their flowers boiled in water."

Whatever their heritage, there was no argument among colonial Americans about the nutritional value of soups. Julianne Belote, author of *The Complete American Housewife,* wrote in 1776:

A good hot soup or broth bubbling in the pot is ever welcome. It soothes the stomach and encourages it to receive more nourishment. It is satisfying for people who are hungry, as well as for those who are tired, worried, cross, in debt, in love or in pain. Even a useless piece of meat can be used if you boil it, extract all its juices and serve a stimulating broth.

Sometimes, apparently, this "stimulating broth" could be pretty thin fare: a weak, watery liquid of the sort Abraham Lincoln characterized as a "homeopathic soup that was made by boiling the shadow of a pigeon that had been starved to death." Despite Lincoln's complaint — which, given the habit of using scant and wilted leftovers to make broth, may have been accurate more often than not — the American idea of soup remained pretty much as Belote describes it: a hot, healthy, economical liquid prepared by simmering "useless" leftovers for long periods.

There were, of course, a number of American soups that owed their fame to much more careful and well-conceived culinary practices. Baltimore, for instance, was well known

Above and opposite: Souvenir postcards featuring the Campbell Kids, c. 1910.

for its turtle soup, prepared from Chesapeake Bay diamondback terrapins. Philadelphia also boasted a kind of turtle soup, claiming that its cream sauce version was infinitely better than the clear, butter- and sherry-laced Baltimore variety. The Pennsylvania Dutch were also good soup makers, corn-and-chicken soup being one of their best known recipes.

Despite these regional specialties, however, soups in early America, as James Beard wrote, were basically "functional" stews, gumbos, or chowders that utilized locally available meats or fish, or they were simply economical ways to use up kitchen scraps. Highly seasoned, carefully prepared soups of the sort that Escoffier considered examples of the fine art of French cuisine were practically unknown in America — and these were precisely the kinds of soup that John Dorrance

hoped to introduce to the American public. In his mind, soup was not simply a practical and healthy dish; it was a delicacy, to be prepared as such and to be eaten like any other fine food. This notion would have lasting consequences for the Joseph Campbell Company.

Dorrance's initial idea about the manufacture of soup — that condensing it by cutting its liquid content in half would drop its price sharply — was in purely commercial terms his most brilliant. But if his conception of soup had stopped there, in all likelihood his product would not have enjoyed the success that it did. Dorrance also had to create a full product line, a list of soups that would appeal to the

American public. This he did with considerable commercial and culinary astuteness.

Within five years of his introduction of its first five soups, the Joseph Campbell Company had expanded its line to include twenty-one varieties. (It is not clear what was magical about the number twenty-one, but despite occasional additions and subtractions, for the next thirty years the company manufactured exactly that number of soups.) The initial repertoire of Campbell's Soups would probably have pleased Escoffier. (All, with the exception of Mock Turtle and Pepper Pot, are included in his famous 1904 cookbook *A Guide to the Fine Art of French Cuisine.*) When advertised, these first soups were usually listed alphabetically: Asparagus, Beef, Bouillon, Celery, Chicken, Chicken

Gumbo, Clam Bouillon, Clam Chowder, Consommé, Julienne, Mock Turtle, Mulligatawny, Mutton, Oxtail, Pea, Pepper Pot, Printanier, Tomato, Tomato Okra, Vegetable, Vermicelli-Tomato.

That most of the soups on this list are instantly recognizable today belies the fact that the makeup of this initial product line was really quite revolutionary. Its creation was the result of a careful and sophisticated understanding of the history, taxonomy, and character of soup. When deciding which varieties to offer, Dorrance had at least a couple of goals in mind. First

of all, he wanted to convince Americans to serve routinely high-quality, rich, and well-prepared soups. Though ease of preparation and price were major attractions of Campbell's Condensed Soups, taste was probably even more important. No matter how inexpensive and convenient, people would not continue to eat the product if its taste were not appealing.

Dorrance's major competitors in this taste-test battle were not other manufacturers but consumers themselves, the American housewives who would compare the product to their own homemade soups. This was an odd rivalry, which in effect pitted the pride of the housewife against the reputation of Campbell's chefs. Dorrance's strategy in this battle was ingenious. First, he manufactured soups that tasted good and were as appealing to the palate as those he had eaten on the Continent. This ensured that, once tried, his product would be bought again. He then suggested that, since making soup at home was such a labor-intensive process, in most cases there was no reason for the

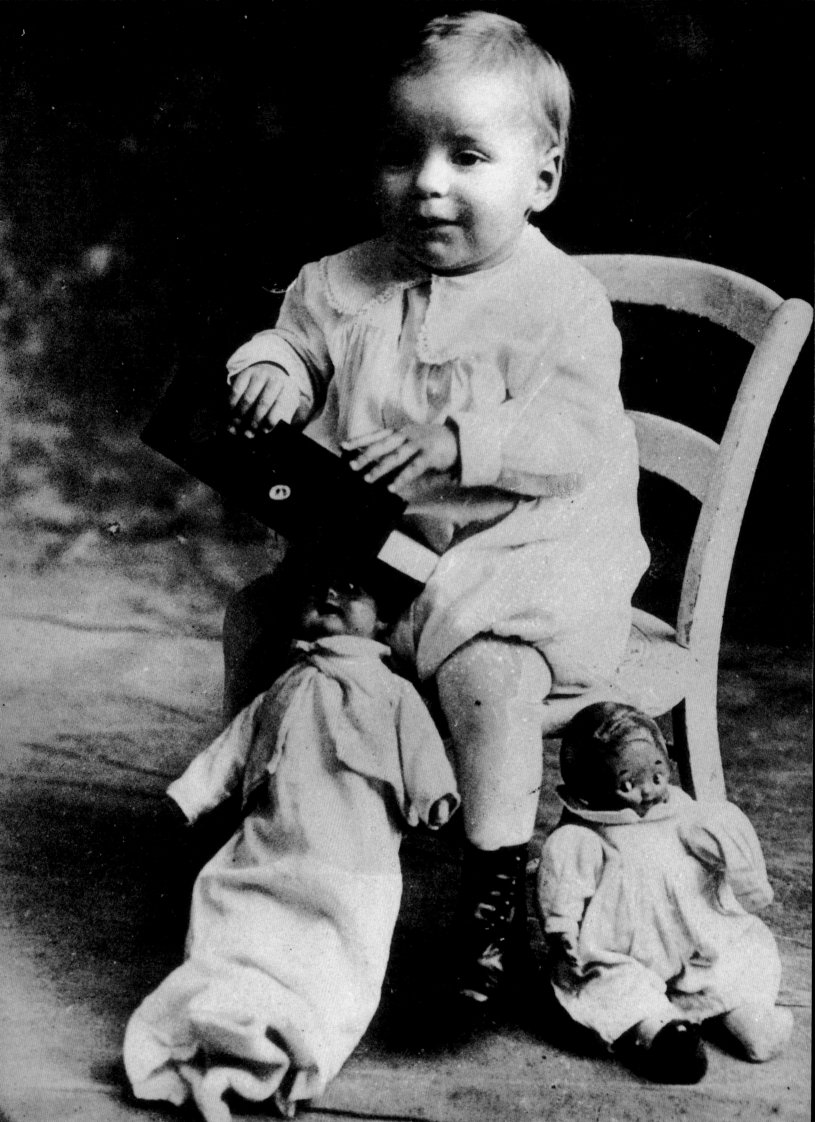

housewife to bother. Thus, Campbell's Soups were presented as an inexpensive delicacy, as good as if not better than homemade soups, and since they came in a can, they were also easier to prepare.

Dorrance also wanted to sell his product in quantity. He wanted to persuade people to eat his soup regularly, at least once a day if possible. To accomplish this second objective, it was necessary to create good soups with which the public could be comfortable; it would not do to have a product that confused or confounded the American palate. If one looks carefully at this first group of soups and analyzes its clever and considered design, it is clear that the initial list was a masterpiece, a product line so well put together that each item played its own role in enhancing the appreciation, and thus the sales, of Campbell's Condensed Soups.

First, there was the careful merging of American and Continental cooking traditions. Almost half of the soups either have a specifically American heritage or are so familiar that one would not have been surprised to find them on the average American table. Beef, Chicken, and Vegetable head this list; each is so patently well known as to have almost no national pedigree. Though the tomato was a New World product, it, too, was common enough in most parts of the world to be considered a standard soup vegetable.

Clam Chowder, normally associated with the clam banks of New England, and Pepper Pot, which was invented in Philadelphia, are also clearly American dishes. (Clam Bouillon as well, despite its French name, has American roots.) Likewise, Mock

Turtle seems to have been created to make up for the unavailability in many parts of the country of the real thing: ocean-going terrapin. Then there are Chicken Gumbo and Tomato Okra, two soups whose stocks are rendered notably American by the addition of okra, a native American vegetable normally associated with Louisiana cuisine.

The other half of the soups that made up the initial twenty-one kinds were, without doubt, relative strangers on the American table. Two of these were either British (Mutton) or had British associations (Mulligatawny). The rest were French in origin, a fact that would not then have endeared them to American eaters. Traditionally, Americans considered French cooking so much fancy frippery. When Thomas

Opposite and above: Children posing with Campbell Kid dolls. Below: French-born Charles Louis De Lisle, Campbell's first executive chef.

Jefferson brought a French cook back
from Paris after his service there as
ambassador, Patrick Henry accused
him of "abjuring his native victuals,"
and an early American cookbook
writer, Mrs. Hannah Glasse, fulminated
against "the blind folly of this age,
that would rather be imposed upon by
a French booby, than give encourage-
ment to a good English cook."

All of this anger and anxiety was,
of course, not equal to any real threat
of a wholesale invasion of French
cooking; the majority of American
housewives went right on cooking
honest Anglo-American fare as they
had always done. In his own way,
John Dorrance hoped to alter, if not
eradicate, this prejudice. In the first
place, all of his soups, no matter what
their national derivation, were cooked
following French culinary operations,
something that would ensure that
each received the care commonly
accorded to French dishes. No more
would meat and vegetable scraps,
along with the few herbs and spices
available, be haphazardly flung into

a pot and simmered. Dorrance's
training at the best American and
French restaurants guaranteed that the
classic recipes would be followed and
that the best cooking techniques would
be strictly adhered to. Even typically
American soups such as Clam Chowder
or Tomato Okra were cooked the
French way.

Dorrance, bucking tradition, also
introduced a number of soups that
were quite specifically French in character, if not in origin. Bouillon and
Consommé, for instance, were both
extremely rich broths — stocks, really
— of the sort that Escoffier described
as being "everything in cooking, at
least in French cooking." Similarly, the
thick vegetable soups — Asparagus,
Celery, and Pea — were prepared as
classical French purees or creams.
Other soups, Julienne and Printanier,
even had French names. They, like
Oxtail, were gelatinous soups, a type
Escoffier considered essential to
French cooking.

Dorrance thus was able to present
a product line that was at once cosmopolitan and quite common, one that
nicely blended Fannie Farmer's goal of
combining "English thoroughness and
French art." The effect of this combination of food heritages was to enable
consumers to choose a soup that fitted
their mood and temperament. If an
honest American dish were wanted,
there were Chicken, Beef, and all the
other specifically American soups.
If one wanted to be more daring, there
was Mock Turtle, Mutton, or Oxtail.
Finally, if a housewife wanted to
impress her guests with her sophistication, there were those soups that
carried the aura of Continental culture

Nineteen Hundred and Twenty Three
Will be a glorious year for me
    With lofty ambition
    And Campbell's nutrition
I'll make it one long jubilee!

Aiming high!

Call on our famous chefs and our great kitchens to give you a "lift" every day. Let them help you in the coming year to make your home even brighter and better than it is. Every member of your family will enjoy the delicious and nourishing Campbell's Soups. And they save your time for other things.

Campbell's Vegetable Soup

is a dish of real substantial food—thirty-two ingredients blended with utmost skill. Baby limas, dainty peas, luscious tomatoes, sugary corn, white and sweet potatoes, tasty turnips, Chantenay carrots, snow-white celery, chopped cabbage, alphabet macaroni, fine barley, French leeks, okra, and fresh parsley, with rich beef broth to tempt the appetite. Aim high tonight! Serve this splendid soup!

21 kinds   12 cents a can

There's welcome variety in Campbell's Soups

Every woman knows that variety is the spice of her table. Just try this easy way to begin your meals with "something different" every day for the next two weeks. Order a selection from the 21 different kinds of Campbell's Soups from your grocer. Serve a different soup each day. It's a sure way to make all the meals "go" better.

Campbell's Soups

LOOK FOR THE RED AND WHITE LABEL

Here and opposite: English and European soup tureens of the eighteenth and nineteenth centuries usually indicated in their design or on the finial atop the lid the kind of soup that was to be found therein. These handsome examples are from a collection of soup tureens formed by Campbell in 1970.

and cultivation: Bouillon, Consommé, Julienne, Printanier.

All told, the initial twenty-one soups cleverly intermingled the exotic (Mulligatawny) with the commonplace (Chicken), the foreign (Printanier) with the native (Clam Chowder), the rich and delicate (Consommé) with the substantial and hearty (Vegetable), the gelatinous (Oxtail) with the smooth and creamy (Asparagus), the universal and international (Tomato) with the regional (Tomato Okra). There was a soup for everyone, no matter what the individual preference, habit, or desire. That some of these soups are still produced in great quantities — Tomato and Vegetable, for instance — while others — such as Mulligatawny and Julienne — have vanished is a testament to the breadth of Dorrance's efforts and the challenges that he faced.

Having chosen and created the twenty-one soups, Dorrance still faced one large task: cultivating in the American public the Continental art of soup eating, convincing the average American that soup should precede a meal and that it should be the first course among many. This was a relatively new idea, and even, apparently, among the French it was not one universally shared. As Escoffier wrote, defending the value of the soup course:

I shall not make any lengthy attempt here to refute the arguments of certain autocrats of the dinner-table who, not so many years ago, urged the total abolition of soups. I shall only submit to their notice the following quotation from Grimod de la Reyniere, one of our most illustrious gastronomists: "soup is to a dinner what the porch or gateway is to a building," that is to say, it must not only form the first portion thereof, but it must be so devised as to convey some idea of the whole to which it belongs; or, after the manner of an overture in a light opera, it should divulge what is to be the dominant phrase of the melody throughout. I am at one with Grimod in this, and believe that soups have come to stay. Of all the items on the menu, soup is that which exacts the most delicate, perfect, and the strictest attention, for upon the first impression it gives to the diner the success of the latter part of the meal largely depends.

Certainly in America soup as a first course, though not unheard of, was definitely not the habit of the average family. To educate the public Dorrance began publishing menu books, combining meal planning and recipes. Books of this sort were a relatively new

phenomenon on the American scene, part of the changing vision of the American kitchen. Since colonial days the American housewife had been seen as a dutiful, hardworking manager of the economy of the household. "The grand arcanum of management can be stated in three simple rules: Let every thing be done at a proper time, keep every thing in its proper place and put every thing to its proper use," advised Mary Randolph of Virginia.

As the twentieth century opened, however, the housewife, then as now the primary provider of a family's meal, was increasingly pictured as one whose great skills and responsibilities deserved broader recognition. This trend toward a greater consideration of the housewife's role in the kitchen was accompanied by a new sophistication about food itself. In the early 1890s Sarah Tyson Rorer, who, like Dorrance, had developed a love for French food after visiting the Continent, opened a cooking school in Philadelphia devoted to the practice of preparing the best-tasting and most nutritious meals possible. (Mrs. Rorer considered bad cooking to be behind the "crowded conditions in our insane asylums, almshouses, prisons and hospitals.") Like Fannie Farmer, who a few years later would publish her famous *Boston Cooking School Cookbook*, Rorer pictured herself as a culinary missionary of sorts, even going so far as to put together a menu book that outlined an entire year's meals. The formulation of a varied, good-tasting,

TUESDAY — TENTH MENU

BREAKFAST
Fruit
Oatmeal   Sugar and Cream
Broiled Tripe   Latticed Potatoes
Pop Overs   Coffee

LUNCHEON
Fried Soft Clams   Sauce Tartare
Fruit   Cake   Cocoa

DINNER
CAMPBELL'S MULLIGATAWNY SOUP
Broiled Steak   Mashed Potatoes   Spinach
Escarole   French Dressing
Wafers   Cheese
Raspberry Foam
Coffee

To keep the blood in good condition various acids and salts are needed. The latter we find in green vegetables, the former in fruits. With the many kinds of evaporated fruits on the market, it is always possible to have some sort of fruit served for breakfast no matter what the season. Remember that evaporated fruits should be well washed, then soaked in fresh cold water for at least twelve hours; they should be slowly cooked in a double boiler until tender and sugar added just before taking from the fire. To have the breakfast bread really "pop over" beat three eggs, add a pint of milk; mix part of this with a pint of sifted flour and a half teaspoonful of salt and beat the thick batter until smooth; dilute this with the remainder of the liquid and strain into deep buttered cups. Have the oven moderately hot so that they scarcely begin to rise for the first twenty minutes. They need almost an hour's baking and, when rightly done, will be three times their first size, hollow and light as a feather.

There are many who consider a dish of fried soft clams incomplete without sauce tartare. This is quickly made by adding two large tablespoonfuls of chopped and squeezed pickled cucumbers and capers to a half cupful of mayonnaise dressing.

As described in cook books, Mulligatawny Soup requires considerable effort and time. CAMPBELL'S MULLIGATAWNY SOUP is ready for use and you just add hot water and serve after a moment's boiling.

As an easy dessert, whip the whites of three eggs to a stiff meringue with three tablespoonfuls of sifted powdered sugar, then gradually beat in a half tumbler of raspberry jelly. The result is delightful but it must not be allowed to stand long before serving.

The distinctive savor of CAMPBELL'S MULLIGATAWNY SOUP is obtained by skillful blending of imported Indian curry powder. Its basis is chicken and rice, with chutney and other condiments added; also fresh fruits, apples, citron, cocoanut etc. The very high seasoning renders this a most delightful soup to those who like the taste of curry.

Additional recipes will be found on pages following menus.

14

WEDNESDAY — ELEVENTH MENU

BREAKFAST
Fruit
Hominy   Sugar and Cream
Creamed Dried Beef   Hashed Potatoes
Crumpets   Coffee

LUNCHEON
Corned Beef Hash   Pickles
Cinnamon Buns   Cocoa

DINNER
CAMPBELL'S PEA SOUP
Breaded Veal Cutlets   Brown Tomato Sauce
Mashed Potatoes   Creamed Carrots
Water Cress   French Dressing
Wafers   Cheese
Date Pudding   Foamy Sauce
Coffee

The sponge for crumpets must be set at night. Dissolve in a pint of scalded milk two tablespoonfuls of butter and a scant teaspoonful of salt; when partly cooled add one-third of an yeast cake dissolved in a little warm water and sufficient sifted flour to make a thin drop batter; beat well and let stand until morning. Heat and grease the griddle; lay greased crumpet rings on it and pour into each sufficient of the light batter to fill two-thirds full. Bake slowly so that the crumpets will color on the underside in from six to eight minutes; turn, slip off the rings and brown on the other side. They are to be torn open, a bit of butter slipped in each and sent at once to the table.

A delightful variation of the usual brown gravy served with chops, cutlets and meats in general may be quickly obtained by using two-thirds stock or water and one-third CAMPBELL'S TOMATO SOUP. The butter or dripping and flour should be carefully browned together and the liquid then gradually added. CAMPBELL'S PEA SOUP is made from fresh green peas, is well flavored and ready to serve in a minute. All these points unite in making it an ideal dinner soup. To any good recipe for batter pudding, add a cupful or more of dates which have been steamed until tender, then pitted and halved. This is an excellent simple fruit pudding.

Pea Soup ordinarily is easily prepared, though seldom appetizing or inviting. CAMPBELL'S PEA SOUP is another kind. Selected fresh green peas, being boiled, are rubbed through fine colanders, then blended with milk, and condiments. Campbell's is essentially a pea soup, containing form and prepared in season only. When preparing, cream should be used instead of water.

Above: Pages from "Campbell's Menu Book." Right: Cover from "Campbell's Menu Book."

healthy diet could be taught, and housewives bought these new cookbooks by the thousands.

The *Campbell's Menu Book*, then, was not without precedent. Indeed, in mirroring the foray of Rorer and Farmer into the world of cultivated and cosmopolitan food preparation, the booklet was actually in the forefront of current food thinking. The introduction explained the reason for it as follows:

The ambitious housewife, confronted daily with the necessity for catering to the capricious appetites of her household — no inconsiderable task even to the resourceful — a collection of menus such as are here presented, offering not only an arrangement of viands in appetite-tempting manner and variety so essential to success, but with due regard to economic value will, we believe, at once commend itself and prove a valuable aid to every woman interested in culinary topics.

This forty-eight-page booklet contained ninety menus, three each for the thirty days of a month. Most of the dishes listed were American in charac-

Below: For the preparation of beef stock, which was the basis for many soups, the Campbell plant in Camden maintained a considerable staff of expert butchers.

You would be the happiest giver alive

—if you could hang the gift of health on every branch of your home Christmas tree this year. But do you realize that eating good soup every day is one of the surest means to bring this priceless gift into your home and keep it there?

And you needn't wait for Santa Claus.

Every time you serve Campbell's nourishing and appetizing Tomato Soup on your home table you help to cultivate the habit of health in the family circle.

Isn't this the finest gift of all?

Made of the pure juice of sound red-ripe tomatoes and other choice and nutritious ingredients, this tempting soup so strengthens digestion, so helps to regulate the body-building processes of the entire system that it proves as wholesome and satisfying as it is delicious.

Write for Campbell's "Helps for the Hostess" book, which describes various inviting ways to serve this delightful soup, beside many new menus and original recipes, which are in themselves a prize well worth having. Free on request.

21 kinds   **15c a can**

"I love this Campbell's Christmas tree
Which grows so green and tall.
Of many joys it brings to me
This gift is best of all"

Campbell's SOUPS
LOOK FOR THE RED AND WHITE LABEL

ter: meat, potatoes, eggs, cereal, bread, cakes, coffee. But into this routine mix of familiar food it attempted to introduce three new culinary ideas: the serving of a hearty soup as the foundation of a light luncheon; flavorful soup as an appetizing first dinner course; and tasty, slightly exotic new dishes to follow and complement that first soup course. For instance, the suggested menu for a typical Monday, the first day of the work week, included:

BREAKFAST
Fruit
Corn Meal Mush
Sugar and Cream
Poached Eggs
Hashed Potatoes
Rice Muffins
Coffee

LUNCHEON
Campbell's Oxtail Soup
Corn Oysters
Pim Olas
Preserves
Cake
Cocoa

DINNER
Campbell's Vermicelli-Tomato Soup
Curry of Mutton
Mashed Potatoes
String Beans
Lettuce
French Dressing
Wafers
Cheese
Junket
Coffee

The breakfast, though large by current standards, would actually have seemed quite small to turn-of-the-century American families. As the introductory material to the menu book explains, the "heavy and abundant first meal of the day" has been "very properly curtailed and instead has been planned with wholesome and sustaining breakfasts that provide — with least digestive discomfort — the vigor demanded by the exigencies of the busy day." Luncheon is also light, characterized by "a daintiness that goes hand in hand with nutriment." Despite the fact that lunch included deep-fried corn oysters, this is basically a light soup-and-sandwich meal, one in which the strong and nourishing oxtail soup is rounded out by the fritters, cake, and preserves.

The dinner menu is a much different matter. It is, the menu book explains,

Below: Cover of Campbell's Tomato Soup recipe booklet, published in 1914. Left: Ads for soup also promoted the availability and use of the Campbell recipe and menu booklets.

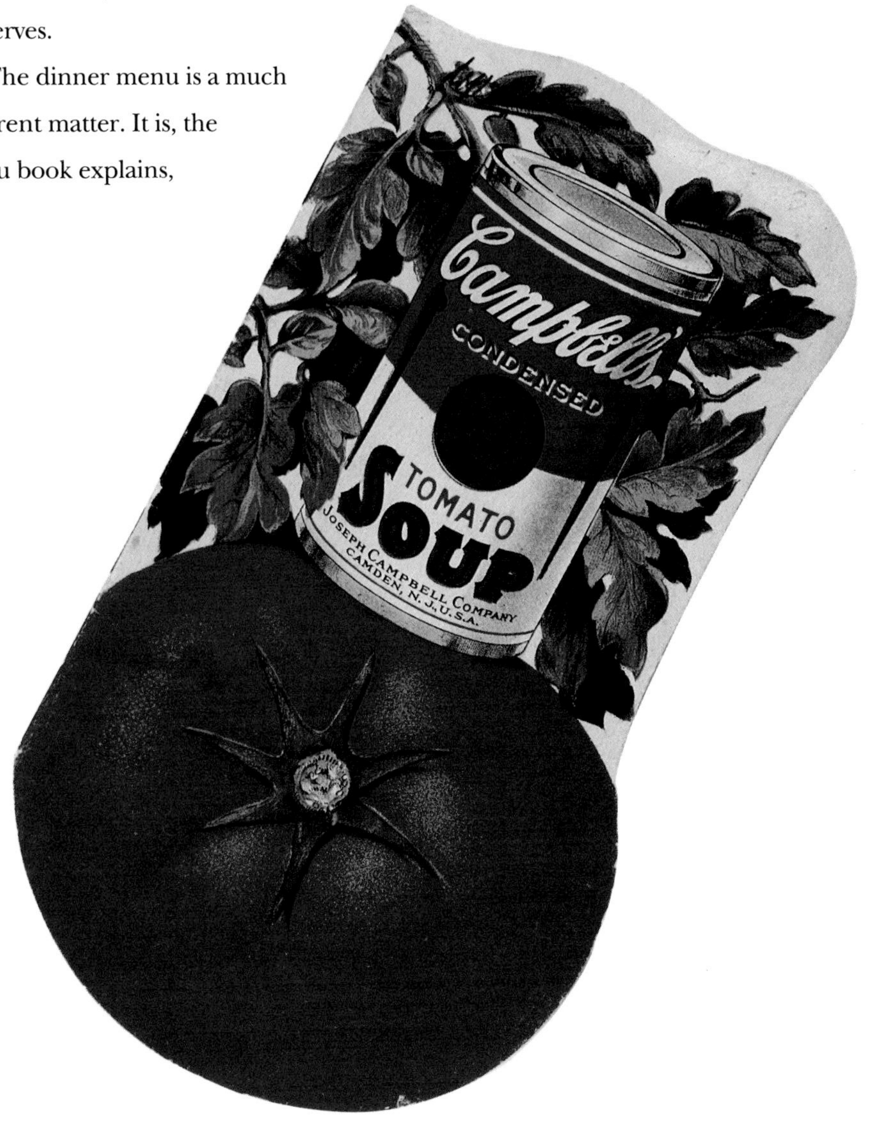

Below: Pages from "Campbell's Helps for the Hostess." Opposite: Cover from "Campbell's Helps for the Hostess," offered to the public in 1916.

"the one meal that is eaten at leisure with care and worry laid aside. . . . It is at dinner the hearty appetite may be indulged with impunity and the menus for this are sufficiently varied and complete to satisfy every reasonable desire." The first course, Escoffier's "gateway" to the meal, is Vermicelli-Tomato, a rich, full soup, which, the menu book argues, "prepares the palate for the curried mutton." This entree, of course, was probably new to the average housewife, and so a recipe was given: "A thick sauce is made with two tablespoons each of butter and flour, a teaspoon of curry powder, a tablespoon of chopped onion, a cupful and a quarter of mutton stock and salt and pepper to taste."

Clearly, the main purpose of this menu was to sell soup. (On this particular day two servings would be con-

sumed.) To do this, as is quite obvious, it strongly encouraged the habit of eating soup as a first dinner course and as a pillar of a good lunch. But in conjunction with these two aims, the booklet also attempted to educate the American housewife, to give her not only healthy and nutritious menus but also dishes, such as curry of mutton, that were new and perhaps slightly exotic. This additional goal is even more conspicuous in one of the booklet's typical Sunday menus.

◆◆◆

BREAKFAST

Fruit

Corn Meal Mush

Sugar and Cream

Broiled Bacon

Stewed Potatoes

Entire Wheat Germs

Coffee

•

DINNER

Campbell's Consommé

Stuffed Veal Shoulder

Brown Gravy

Mashed Potatoes

Asparagus Tips

Chicory Salad

Wafers

Cheese

Caramel Custard

Coffee

•

SUPPER

Creamed Soft Clams in the Chafing Dish

Nut Sandwiches

Layer Cake

Bavarian Cream

Coffee

◆◆◆

AFTER THEATER SUPPER

MENU No. 22

Campbell's Bouillon with small pilot crackers
Chilaly
Bacon sandwiches
Frosted orange squares

BACON SANDWICHES: Broil or fry as many bacon strips as sandwiches desired. Have ready circles of rye bread, spread with butter to which one-quarter teaspoonful French mustard is added. Place bacon between two slices, press together, and serve instantly.

CHILALY
1 tablespoonful butter.
½ teaspoonful dry mustard and salt.
1 teaspoonful Worcestershire sauce.
2 tablespoonfuls chopped green pepper.
1 tablespoonful chopped onion.
¼ cup CAMPBELL'S TOMATO SOUP.
¼ pound sharp cheese run through chopper.
2 tablespoonfuls milk.
1 egg.

Cook butter with onions and pepper until brown. Rub mustard and salt together, add to TOMATO SOUP, then add to butter mixture. Boil up, add cheese and Worcestershire. When cheese is melted, add milk, and egg slightly beaten. Serve at once on hot pilot crackers. This is best cooked in the blazer of a chafing dish.

CHILDREN'S SUPPERS

Cream of Campbell's Chicken Soup
Steamed whitefish
Baked potato
Cup custard, strawberry sauce
Steamed spinach
Oatmeal cookies

Cream of Campbell's Celery Soup
Panned chopped round steak
Creamed carrots
Stewed figs
Chocolate cornstarch
Gingerbread

38

INFORMAL LUNCHEON

MENU No. 23

Campbell's Celery Soup Bisque
Toasterettes
Green corn, Creole style
Raspberry short cake
Iced coffee cup

GREEN CORN, CREOLE STYLE
2 cups corn kernels cut from cob.
1 cup CAMPBELL'S TOMATO SOUP.
4 tablespoonfuls butter.
4 tablespoonfuls flour.
1 teaspoonful salt.
1 tablespoonful onion juice.
2 tablespoonfuls chopped green pepper.
1 tablespoonful chopped parsley.

Melt butter and in it cook the pepper until tender. Add the flour, blend, and add tomato soup. Stir until smooth. Then add seasonings and corn, heat thoroughly, and serve at once.

RASPBERRY SHORTCAKE
3 cups flour.
3 teaspoonfuls baking powder.
½ teaspoonful salt.
½ cup butter.

Mix thoroughly, then add sufficient milk to form dough. Divide dough into two parts, and roll each part out on buttered pan. Spread top of each with softened butter, and fit one over the other. Bake twenty minutes in hot oven. Remove top layer and return both layers to the oven a few minutes to form slight crust. Take from oven, butter both crusts, place layer of berries on the lower one, sift with soft sugar, add top layer, pipe edges with whipped cream and pile top of cake with berries. Crush extra berries, add sugar and melted butter, place in pan of hot water to keep warm, and pour over separately.

39

HELPS
FOR THE
HOSTESS

Below: This production line of
huge kettles served in the preparation of consommé and stocks for
other soups.

In America the traditional Sunday dinner is eaten not in the evening, but at midday. Here that meal, though essentially a typical mix of meat, potatoes, and vegetables, begins with a plate of consommé. Recognizing that the inclusion of a soup course in a Sunday dinner is a little unconventional, the booklet argues that "there is no need to omit soup from the Sunday dinner when any of the Campbell varieties are in the house," and then, like the most knowledgeable expert, recommends "a clear soup — Campbell's Consommé." The notes that accompany this meal provide a recipe for the entree: "The veal shoulder is boned and the cavity filled with a stuffing made by mixing one quart of finely crumbled stale bread with three chopped onions, a half a cup of melted veal or beef drippings and a high seasoning of salt and pepper."

The *Campbell's Menu Book* was clearly written with the average family in mind. As a rule, its meals are relatively conservative and its forays into haute cuisine limited to dishes such as curry of mutton, veal shoulder, and creamed soft clams. For the most part, the entrees are fairly conventional: steamed cod, roast loin of pork, baked fresh ham, meat pie. However, another Campbell's menu booklet of the time, *Helps for the Hostess*, goes much further into the realm of formal and fine dining. This is the guide for those, the booklet's introduction states, who believe that "a well-chosen, well-prepared menu is a creator of appetite; a promoter of good digestion and health. A refined, well-appointed home table," the booklet continues, "gives a recognized social standing, which money alone will not achieve, among people who are worthwhile." In other words, money is not the sole measure of good taste. "Such a table," it is argued, "is entirely within reach of moderate means."

Unlike the *Campbell's Menu Book*, which is organized by day of the week, the forty-three menus and one hundred recipes in *Helps for the Hostess* are grouped into seven main classes: formal and informal dinners, formal and informal luncheons, Sunday suppers, after-theater suppers, and chafing dish suppers. The formal dinner is the touchstone, the most revealing of all these meals.

To give a successful formal dinner is perhaps the highest test of the social skill and ability of the hostess. It permits her to express her taste and refinement not only in the choice of the all-important menu,

Below: A visionary plan of
Dr. Dorrance's for a new industrial
park centered on a Campbell
factory complex proved impractical
and was abandoned. The development of regional plants closer
to consumers in other parts of the
country proved to be a better
solution.

but in the details of table setting and service. A formal dinner may consist of from six to ten or more courses. The success of such a function does not depend upon the elaborateness of the menu but upon its quality and the correctness and excellence of the service in all its details.

Having said this, the next four pages of *Helps for the Hostess* lay out in detail what is, in effect, a short primer on the presentation of food. While most families eat "English style, in which the host and hostess carve and serve part of the meal directly at the table," this will not do for formal dinners, which must be served "à la Russe," from the side, "by attendants who pass it to each guest in individual portions direct from the pantry or side table."

The table also must be laid correctly, for this is "the starting point of a successful dinner." Fifteen rules are given, each of which must be followed if the meal is to be a triumph of good taste. For instance:

Allow twenty-five to thirty inches in width for each individual "cover." Allow fifteen inches in depth for each cover; i.e., all plates, silver, etc., must be set within an imaginary line fifteen inches from the edge of the table.

The service plate is the center of each cover; and all plates, cutlery and silver must be set one-half inch from the edge of the table. Place at the right of the service plate the dinner knife (cutting edge toward the plate); then the entree knife; then the soup spoon (bowl up) beyond and parallel; last a canape or oyster fork (tines up) across the soup spoon (with tines pointing toward the service plate).

THE NORTH AMERICAN

MAGAZINE (Sixth) SECTION

PHILADELPHIA, SUNDAY, APRIL 11, 1915.

CAMPBELLTOWN, A FORETASTE OF INDUSTRIAL UTOPIA

Opposite: Campbell's prepared soups invaded the tradition-bound European market with considerable success, and by the 1930s a continental distri-butor could boast that he had "shipped" Campbell soups even into rural Sweden, proof of which he offered by sending the photograph opposite to company headquarters.

Additional information is given on serving an informal dinner with only one maid, a formal luncheon and an informal dinner without a maid. In this last case, everything should "be placed in readiness, so that the hostess need arise as little as possible."

The food for these meals reflects an equal cultivation and polish. Menu No. 1, for a formal dinner, is as follows:

◆◆◆

Oysters on half-shell

Celery stuffed with caviar

Campbell's Tomato Soup

Toast triangles

Stuffed turbans of flounder

Potatoes Parisienne

Breast of guinea fowl with currant sauce

Pimento grapefruit salad

Peach Plombière

Demi-tasse

Cheese fingers

◆◆◆

It is not clear, of course, how many of the millions of cans of Campbell's soups were served in this fashion, but Dorrance had effected an almost revolutionary change in national eating habits. Almost overnight America became a nation of canned-soup eaters. By 1907, ten years after the introduction of Campbell's Condensed Soups, sales topped one million dollars for the first time. And each year that figure grew amazingly quickly, reaching twelve million dollars by the beginning of World War I.

How can one account for this incredible growth? Certainly Dorrance's marketing and advertising were important. Without them Campbell's Soups would not have reached the public as they did. But it was the soups themselves that were the most important factor in their own success. Prepared as culinary delicacies, they were so consistently good-tasting that they were considered a gold standard of sorts. They were not compared with homemade soups; they were something slightly different with a taste all their own. They were *Campbell's* soups. And for that culinary accomplishment, Dorrance's brilliance in the choice and preparation of each soup was primarily responsible.

The 21 Kinds

Members of the Dorrance family liked to joke that Dr. John Dorrance — the holder of a doctorate in organic chemistry and by 1915 the sole owner of a company that grossed $9.5 million a year — was a man completely "in love with soup." Indeed, he once remarked that his prime ambition in life was to manage his company so successfully that it would grow to be the largest manufacturer of soup in the United States.

Dorrance met his goal relatively quickly, both by hard work and a determined and obsessive business savvy. Less than twenty years after he went to work for his uncle as a $7.50-a-week industrial chemist, he was in complete charge of every facet of the company: manufacturing, marketing, sales, even the incoming mail, which for many years he personally opened each

morning in order, he said, always to keep abreast of consumer response to his products.

In some ways Dorrance was not the typical turn-of-the-century industrial magnate. He was neither flamboyant nor ostentatious. He espoused no causes, publicly or privately. He was at heart a shy, studious, intellectual man, not the sort to wear his wealth on his sleeve. In his entire life Dorrance's name appeared in the *New York Times* on only three occasions, and then only in passing. Even today, most people associate the company with Joseph Campbell, a man who concluded his association with the firm in 1900 and had next to nothing to do with its entry into the soup business.

After marrying Ethel Malinckrodt, a Baltimore socialite, in 1906, Dorrance and his wife lived first in a modest

Camden apartment not far from his office. In 1911, after the birth of their first two children, they moved into a large but unpretentious brick home on a 176-acre farm in Cinnaminson, New Jersey, nine miles from the plant. In the front yard of the house which he rented from the Joseph Campbell Company, Dorrance planted and tended tomatoes, always looking for the perfect strain to make into Tomato Soup. Eventually, as his family grew to four daughters and a son, Dorrance moved across the river to a mansion in Radnor, Pennsylvania, on the fashionable Main Line outside Philadelphia. But even then he kept the Cinnaminson farm where, it was said, he was more comfortable.

By all accounts, Dorrance was an extremely orderly businessman. He ran his company, he said, as if it had

the fiduciary responsibilities of a bank. Each of the firm's departments was required to keep records of income and outgo, which were checked daily as a bank teller tallies a cash drawer. Not a cent was left unaccounted for. On the eighteenth of each month, three days after the books were closed, Dorrance himself was given a summary balance sheet covering practically every transaction made by the company, which he then painstakingly audited to keep close track of what was growing into a hugely profitable enterprise.

At the time Dorrance began manufacturing and marketing his products, the American grocery business was in a state of transition. As the United States became increasingly urban and populous, the small owner-operated general store, which had been supplied with goods by local wholesalers and rack jobbers, began to be replaced by chain grocery stores. These large corporate enterprises such as the A & P Company were big and powerful enough to integrate both wholesaling and retailing under one roof. The buying power of these chains and their concomitant ability to sell food at a discount were so enormous that they threatened to put the smaller mom-and-pop corner stores completely out of business.

Dorrance, however, was not cowed by the competitive advantages of the large chains which could, if they wanted, demand deep discounts and undercut their competitors by selling soup at prices the smaller stores could not match. He made the decision to treat each of his clients alike, no matter what its size. This policy was certainly ethical, but it was also very good business. As Dorrance once said, his goal was to see his product on the shelves of every grocery store in the nation. Wherever and whenever a customer wanted to buy a can of soup, Campbell's had to be available.

At the time, however, many large chains were selling nationally advertised brands such as Campbell's at little, if any, markup from the wholesale price. If the big retailers passed this saving on to the consumer as a loss leader, the smaller operators, being unable to compete, might just drop Campbell's Soup from their shelves. To prevent this, which might have resulted in the selling of less soup, each of the company's distributors received exactly the same discount and was held to the same credit requirements. Though some dealers grumbled about these policies, Dorrance was firm, and he could afford to be; before 1920 Campbell's Soup had become so popular that no wholesaler or retailer could afford not to stock the product. When buying soup, the public pre-

Tomato Soup.

This soup is so well known as to require little explanation. Here again we wish to call attention to the smooth appearance and careful blending of the spices.

Our Tomato Soup is not a sweet soup; it should not be so, and our increasing sales of this variety show that it suits the taste of the majority. Sugar can easily be added when desired. If found rather too thick, the soup can be diluted with Consommé.

We suggest the two following additions:

Croûtons

Take a slice of stale bread; remove the crust, cut the inside part into cubes about half an inch in size and fry briskly in a small quantity of butter (about enough to cover the bottom of the frying pan) until these cubes turn a nice brown color. Take them out with a skimmer and throw them into the soup when serving.

Rice

After thoroughly washing the necessary quantity of rice (a tablespoonful is sufficient for a quart can of soup) put it in a saucepan with plenty of cold water and a pinch of salt. Bring the water to boiling point and let it boil freely for twenty minutes; strain the rice and throw it into the hot soup.

Mulligatawny Soup.

A hot and spicy Indian soup. No less than thirty two varieties of spices and other condiments are used in the making of it, among others, Indian curry, Bengal chutney, mangoes, Cayenne pepper, etc.

The basis is thickened chicken stock, garnished with pieces of chicken and rice.

The soup is a favorite with persons partial to highly seasoned food.

Above: The Campbell experimental farm in Cinnaminson, New Jersey, where John Dorrance once grew tomatoes in the fields surrounding his family home.

ferred the Campbell's brand and, if need be, would cross the street to patronize a store that stocked it.

Dorrance also did not leave the marketing of his product up to the retailer. In fact, the firm had a relatively small sales department of only several hundred, compared to the thousand or more employed by other large companies. Most of these salesmen had no office; they simply traveled the country by car, carrying hot samples in thermos bottles. Often, especially in rural areas, customers had never heard of some of Campbell's kinds of soups, and this occasionally caused some confusion. Once, for instance, the owner of a country grocery store came out of the back room with an open can of the recently introduced Black Bean Soup, which, he said, a customer had returned. The Campbell's salesman asked what

the complaint was. "Look at it," the store owner said, peering into the can, "it's black." The salesman did not know what to say except to agree that, yes, it was black, it was Black Bean Soup!

As valuable as these salesmen were, Campbell needed relatively few of them. Unlike many manufacturers of the era who felt they had to convince dealers to carry their products, Dorrance preferred to let the customer do the convincing. This he did by creating a demand for his soups through advertising. Though advertising is now so commonplace that it is hard to imagine marketing without it, at the time using national advertising as the primary method of promoting a product was a relatively new idea.

Campbell's soups were first advertised primarily on streetcar cards, visible to millions of potential buyers each day, but by 1905 it had become

clear that the pages of newspapers and magazines were also extremely effective places to promote Campbell's products. For a few years Campbell's advertising was fairly evenly divided among car cards, newspapers, and magazines. By 1914 the use of cards had become limited to only a few major cities, and newspaper advertising had been dropped completely, the feeling being that neither of these methods of advertising was as effective as magazine ads.

Most of the company's advertising dollar was spent on ads in mass-market magazines such as the *Saturday Evening Post* and *American Magazine*, which were most likely to reach the principal purchaser of soup, the housewife. To

◆◆◆

Opposite: Campbell salesmen pose on the roof of the Camden plant in 1909. Below: Campbell's twenty-one kinds of soup, 1931.

ensure that these ads were seen by all who read the magazine, Dorrance instructed the advertising agency handling his account, F. Wallace Armstrong of Philadelphia, to insist that all Campbell's ads be "the first advertisement following solid text, on a right hand page facing a full page of text." Armstrong and his associate, L. Ward Wheelock, were so successful in this effort that this location became known — and is still known — in the advertising community as the "Campbell's Soup position."

Campbell's Soup also played a starring role in one of the first efforts at market research. The Curtis Publishing Company, which put out the *Ladies Home Journal* and *Saturday Evening Post*, decided that it needed to know which products its readers actually bought after seeing ads in one of its magazines. In 1911 Curtis hired a former schoolteacher from Wisconsin, Charles Coolidge Parlin, to devise market-research methods. One of Parlin's best known attempts to ascertain what people purchased became known as the "Ash and Trash Survey." Fifty-six Philadelphia subscriber families of varied socioeconomic backgrounds agreed to let him go through their trash and record what he found. Approximately six thousand packages were identified, a significant number of which were Campbell's Soup cans.

After receiving the results of the survey, Dorrance discovered two very important facts: first, that advertising in magazines such as the *Ladies Home Journal* was extremely effective — it was not just coincidence that readers of the magazine were also soup buyers. Second, and perhaps even more importantly, the study suggested that Campbell's soups knew no class. Everyone, regardless of income, ate one or more of the twenty-one varieties.

This latter discovery altered and broadened the company's advertising message. Previously, Campbell's ads, as evidenced by company-produced booklets such as *Helps for the Hostess*, had emphasized the elegance and sophistication of soup, assuming that if the "rich lady on the hill" ate it, other sorts of people would emulate her. What the "Ash and Trash Survey" indicated, however, was that Campbell's Soup was a product whose appeal was so widespread that it was unnecessary to target just one class of consumer. In fact, its consumers formed a group about as wide as one could imagine: American housewives.

As a group, housewives stood out as a very specialized community of consumers. Unlike many other purchasing groups (those who bought cars or cameras, for instance), the housewife was the maker of the family's daily meals, and she was therefore in direct competition with those, like the Joseph Campbell Company, who prepared

large quantities of food in factory settings. The difference between the home and the industrial kitchen, home cooks thought, was in size, not in kind. Furthermore, it was the unusual housewife who would give the competitive cooking edge to a mere manufacturer. Most felt they could cook as well as anyone, and it was on that basis that their reputations as the providers of their families' meals depended.

One way to attract the attention of this group was magazine advertising; another was to offer the opinion of experts trained in the arts and crafts of the kitchen. These writers, most often women, were following the intellectual lead of Catherine Beecher, Sarah Tyson Rorer, and Fannie Farmer, among others; they were culinary authorities in a position to give advice on the preparation of healthful and good-tasting fare. Some wrote cookbooks, but most of these experts published their work in newspapers and magazines such as the *Ladies Home Journal* that were aimed at a female audience.

Typical of these articles is a long feature from the *New York Tribune* titled

"A Trip to Camden Town and the Far-Famed Kitchen of Joseph Campbell," by Anne Lewis Pierce, whose impressive credentials were described as "Director Tribune Institute, Master of Science, George Washington University, Washington, D.C., Editor in the Bureau of Chemistry and Associate Editor on Good Housekeeping Magazine Bureau of Food and Sanitation and Health — both under Dr. Wiley and Co-Author with Dr. Wiley of '1001 Tests of Foods, Beverages and Cosmetics'."

Pierce entered the Campbell kitchens with three criteria on which she would judge their excellence. "The first thing to consider," she wrote, "is the recipe, the quantity and the quality of the ingredients. The second is the technique in cooking and combining and the third is cleanliness and sanitary surroundings." She was suitably impressed by the quality of the ingredients, as well she might have been, for this was one of Dr. John Dorrance's obsessions. Every ingredient had to be farm fresh and of very high quality. Soup made the old way, with leftover pieces of meat and

"At study, at work or at fun
I go like a Yank at a Hun.
On Campbell's Soup diet, I never stay quiet
But keep every job on the run."

Sergeant Robert Spengler of Springfield, Mass., and comrades of Company K, 104th United States Infantry, famous as the first American regiment to be decorated for bravery by any foreign government. This photograph was taken directly back of the lines in France.

Left: The Campbell Kids went to war in 1918 as the company pitched in to boost morale on the home front. Right: By 1926, in the heart of the Roaring Twenties, color ads in the leading women's magazines dazzled the eye. In magazine editorial features of the day, and for many years thereafter, only black and white illustrations appeared; color was reserved for aggressive advertisers like Campbell.

All the rich tomato goodness is in Campbell's Tomato Soup!

12 cents a can

WITH THE MEAL OR AS A MEAL SOUP BELONGS IN THE DAILY DIET!

Above: The photographs on page 85 and following were made for an article on Campbell that appeared in *Fortune* magazine in 1935. They were taken by Margaret Bourke-White, then just beginning her career. Bourke-White would become one of the great American photojournalists of mid-century, covering events around the world for *Life* magazine before, during, and after World War II. Above: Workers at Campbell's Camden plant wash their hands before preparing carrots for soup.

bunches of wilted vegetables, did not qualify as a gourmet food.

The day Pierce visited the factory, Vegetable Soup was being made. As she described the scene,

[the] long row of girls, scraping vivid yellow carrots, would have tempted a painter, as well as a gourmand; firm, white cabbages, big yellow rutabagas from Canada; corn, tiny lima and small peas (out of small two-pound cans, the fresh June crop, canned under contract for this purpose) were being opened and each can inspected before it was added to the soup.

All the ingredients, she added, were "table quality"; in fact, most of them "you could eat without further cooking!"

Pierce was also impressed by the cleanliness of the Campbell kitchens, no mean achievement given the number of people working side by side and the labor-intensive task of preparing soup. ("Every woman knows what a bugbear the preparation of fresh vegetables is; the time it takes, the amount of refuse that accumulates, and the cleaning up afterward," she wrote.) In addition, at Campbell's, there were the cooking implements to clean and maintain: the Enterprise machines that chopped and mashed; pots such as the 220-gallon broth caldrons and 110-gallon blending kettles, both made of solid nickel; long rows of meat-and-vegetable-preparation tables; the sterilizing retorts into which the filled cans were placed for a final processing. At night, Pierce reported, two hundred workers forced steam through all the machines and scrubbed all floors and surfaces with hot water and baking soda.

What Pierce could not have seen, since it was a trade secret, was the recipe for Vegetable Soup. Actually, Campbell's Soup recipes came in two parts: the list of ingredients with their weights and measurements, and the directions for combining them. The two parts were kept separate to ensure secrecy. Dorrance's personal copy of cooking directions for the Vegetable Soup Pierce watched being made has survived. The care it requires and the tone in which it is written, if not like the standard cookbook recipe, are revealing of his seriousness in matters of soup making.

All weights used in the Soup are net, i.e., beef and ham are weighed after the fat is trimmed from same and the vegetables after they are diced.

Beef. Should be one-half lean beef and the other half heavy bones. The meat and the ham should be cut into pieces not larger than two inches square, which should be placed in the iron kettles (not more than three batches in each kettle) in cold water. After allowing beef to remain in the cold water from fifteen to thirty minutes, steam should gradually be turned on the kettle,

the same taking about one hour or more to come to a boil. During this time the kettles should be skimmed almost constantly. By neglecting this detail, the value of the broth is decreased, hence the quality of the Soup.

After the stock has been cooked from six to eight hours, the trimmings of celery and parsley are placed in the kettle. It is almost impossible to use too large a quantity of either of these materials. This broth is kept simmering until it is time to be used, and as the water evaporates it should be constantly replaced. This meat should be almost in shreds by the time the broth is to be used.

By having placed a screen previously in the bottom of the kettle, one can draw off the broth from the valve without removing the meat.

The Spices, consisting of celery seed, cloves, allspice, three oz. thyme and bay leaves, are treated in a similar manner, as described in Tomato Soup spices. . . . The white and the red pepper, the salt as well as the curry powder are mixed together.

The parsley, which has been previously chopped fine, as well as one oz. cleaned fine thyme are mixed together.

Sweet potatoes, as they are used only for flavoring, are run through the Enterprise machine. The carrots, white potatoes, onions, and turnips are diced.

The broth is now brought down from the broth kettles and is divided according to the number of batches which have been cooked in each kettle. To this is added the tomato pulp, then the diced carrots, turnip, onions, sweet potatoes, cabbage, barley, celery, flageolet beans, and rice. This mixture is then boiled until the carrots and turnips are cooked. The amount in the kettle should now be eighty gallons. Add to the contents of the kettle the spices, sugar, salt, curry powder, and pepper. If fresh okra is used, it is now placed in the kettle. Sugar and the flour paste are added. The contents of the kettle should now be within one inch of the top. Parsley and Worcester Sauce and the alphabets are now added — in placing alphabets later in the kettle care should be taken that they are well stirred and not dumped in, otherwise they will all cake together.

The canned corn, peas, lima beans and okra (if used) are placed in the can in which the Soup is drawn off. This should be thoroughly mixed before placing in cans.

Process forty minutes at a temperature of 240 degrees Fahrenheit.

Could the average woman make such a soup, Pierce asked, for only ten cents a can? The answer was, of course, no, an acknowledgment that Campbell's advertising was attempting to suggest in so many other ways. As the most famous Campbell's advertising jingle of the time had put it:

We blend the best with careful pains
In skillful combination
And every single can contains
Our business reputation.

As sales increased, so did the amount of money spent on advertising. What had begun as a $10,000 allotment in 1899 rose steadily to $50,000 in 1901, $400,000 in 1911, and in 1920 to $1,000,000 (5 percent of total sales). This strategy, which is now routine, was at the time revolutionary. "When you have the consumer sold," Dorrance explained,

Above: A Campbell worker transfers soup from a blending kettle into a can-filling machine. These huge, expensive nickel kettles were especially made for Campbell in Austria. At left: Preparers slice thin strips of cheddar cheese from big wheels for use in soup.

you have finished the worst part of the campaign. If the consumer makes the demand, the dealer will stock, and if the dealer stocks, the jobber is bound to get the business, and if he lists it for the dealer, we have to make the soup, It is perfectly simple and eliminates a complexity of selling methods.

Dorrance was also adamant that the price of his soup — ten cents a can — be as "unalterable as the laws of the Medes and Persians. Any stenographer of any organization," he continued, "could handle the orders for Campbell's Soups, because our price and terms never vary. We advertise the retail price in large letters in our page advertisements."

While it is certainly true that Dorrance devoted much of his attention to the orderly, honest, and extremely profitable running of his business, his great love, as his family joked, was the soup itself: its almostmystical status as the most flavorful, economical, and nutritious food on the market. About soup his zeal was almost that of a missionary.

Early-twentieth-century advertising tended to be rather more forthright than it is today. It was replete with copy, sentence after sentence and paragraph after paragraph of arguments, exhortations, and explanations. Take, for instance, a typical Campbell ad of the time. In a box at the top of the page, bold letters proclaim: "He who makes good soup, or sells it, is a useful citizen. He who eats good soup every day is wise and takes care of his blood and body. Soup is an economical food; it stimulates digestion; it is an essential part of civilization."

Such claims today seem overblown, but give or take some excessive enthusiasm — probably attributable to the pen of an adman — Dorrance almost certainly would have agreed, at least in principle, with the ideas expressed above and with the remainder of the ad, which describes itself as a "brief sermon on soup," presented at an "important gathering of wholesaler grocers of the United States":

The making of soup on a big scale has been reduced to a science in America. The home- made soup is often beyond the reach of people of small means and inconvenient to the rich. Boiling of joints and keeping up of "soup stock" is expensive under Beef Trust government, and awkward in modern homes.

◆◆◆

Below: Careful stirring by hand was for years the only way to keep ingredients properly mixed. Mechanical stirrers tended to make them separate. Right: Soup cans are loaded into a cooker.

DELICACIES IN TINS from the FRANCO-AMERICAN FOOD CO

Above: Cover of Franco-American informational booklet, c. 1910. Below, the bronze medal won by Franco-American in the same year that Campbell won a gold medal for its soup.

But the manufacture of soups on a big and economical scale has been brought to perfection, so that as a food soup is now as economical as it is beneficial.

The individual cook or the big manufacturer that can prepare soup properly and economically is a treasure.

The grocer, wholesale or retail, who encourages the sale of soup is a useful citizen — and can do more for the health of his customers perhaps than the average doctor.

We advise fathers and mothers that do not yet know the value of a most important food to try the experiment of giving soup to their children at least once a day. The warm liquid brings the blood to the stomach and the alimentary canal for the process of digestion in a natural way. A moment's heating suffices to prepare a most important dish.

And when children form the habit of eating soup regularly at the beginning of a meal they are much less apt to form, later, the habit of taking cocktails regularly in order to bring about artificially and harm-

fully a craving for food — which soup creates naturally and beneficially.

This is our sermon to the wholesalers on soup. We advise them to sell as much as possible of it, and we advise you to eat it, once a day, at least.

Though Dr. John Dorrance may not have succeeded in persuading every American to eat soup daily, he had, practically on his own, invented an industry. In the manufacture and sales of canned soup he had no serious competitor; in fact, in the condensed soup business, he had no competition at all. Only the Franco-American Company had any national following, and its prepared foods, being more expensive than Campbell's, were considered specialties that today might be purchased in a gourmet grocery store. It is clear, however, that Dorrance very much admired the products, production methods, and above all, the image of the competitive company.

Franco-American had begun making soup in 1887, when the French émigré Alphonse Biardot and his sons, Ernest and Octave, opened their first commercial kitchen in Jersey City, New Jersey. Alphonse Biardot, an expert in fine dining, had come to America in 1880 after serving in the Greek royal household as resident major domo. His sons had similar expertise: Ernest in the art of French cuisine and Octave in the management of kitchens. The name of the company they created perfectly described its mission: to market foods that would introduce Americans to French traditions of masterful cooking.

Unlike Dorrance, who limited his product line to soup and Pork &

General view of the kitchen, a room 200 feet long with high ceilings finished in hard wood and with maple flooring; windows on all sides and exhaust fans overhead produce fine ventilation.

Above: Franco-American kitchens as illustrated in a Franco-American informational booklet of 1909, entitled "Franco-American Soups – How They Are Made In A Model Establishment."

Beans, the Biardots canned a wide variety of specialty items, all of which were meant to appeal to the cultivated palate. For instance, Franco-American offered six kinds of Truffled Game Pâté: Partridge, Quail, Grouse, Wild Duck, Chicken, and Chicken Liver. Pâté, of course, was not a familiar part of the American diet; few except the rich had even heard of it. The same was true of Franco-American's Ready-made Entrees, which included Chicken à la Provençale, Chicken Sauté à la Marengo, Chicken Curry à l'Indienne, Calf's Tongue, Sauce Piquante, Beef à la Mode, and Beef Burgundy Style.

Today, thanks to the immense popularity of Julia Child and other food personalities, the American public is much more knowledgeable about these sorts of dishes. Television

cooking shows number in the dozens, and the cuisines they attempt to teach range from Chinese to French to regional American, such as Southern and Pennsylvania Dutch. In addition, a rich body of literature specifically about food and cooking has developed. Most bookstores stock a large shelf of texts written by such experts as James Beard, Craig Claiborne, M. F. K. Fisher, and Betty Fussel, and as we shall see, even the prepared-food industry is part of the new culinary sophistication. At the turn of the century, however, even John Dorrance, who could rightly be called a gourmet, at least in the field of soups, seldom strayed as far as Franco-American from the typical American menu.

But Dorrance very much respected Franco-American for having taken

the high culinary route, and he knew that, in its own way, it was a successful commercial enterprise. When his brother Arthur Calbraith Dorrance was looking for a way to learn the food business, John lent him the $650,000 necessary to buy all outstanding Franco-American stock. Purchasing a company is perhaps a rare method of learning a business.

Arthur was the younger of John Dorrance's brothers. His older brother, George Morris Dorrance, who had no interest whatsoever in the food business, had studied medicine at the University of Pennsylvania and become one of Philadelphia's leading onco-logic surgeons. Arthur, who was twenty years younger than John, followed in his brother's footsteps and enrolled in MIT, graduating in 1914 with a bachelor of science degree in chemical engineering. While still a student, Arthur had worked summers in the Campbell plant, and after graduation he joined the company full-time and was given a job in the experimental kitchen. John Dorrance decided that this experience was not enough, so he sent his brother off to train as a soup chef in New York City's Hotel McAlpin.

Arthur was fired from this first job, but he continued his training at the Ritz. It was at this point that, with his brother's loan, he purchased the Franco-American stock. Though Arthur, in effect, owned the company and was actively engaged in it, nominal control remained with Alphonse Biardot. World War I interrupted Arthur Dorrance's active involvement with Franco-American: he joined the army and served honorably as an artillery captain. After the war, he

returned to work, not for Campbell or Franco-American but for another canning company, Gorton-Pew Fisheries of Gloucester County, New Jersey.

It was at this time that Arthur sold John his controlling interest in Franco-American. (This was probably more of a transfer than a sale since he had borrowed the money from him in the first place.) Dorrance then transferred the stock to his wife, Ethel, and by January 1915 he was the owner of two food-manufacturing firms: Joseph Campbell Company and the Franco-American Company.

For a time Franco-American continued operations as usual, manu-facturing ready-to-serve soups and other gourmet products.

In June 1921, however, the board of directors of the Joseph Campbell Company authorized the purchase of Mrs. Dorrance's Franco-American stock, paying exactly the same amount as Arthur had paid the Biardots in 1916. By this exchange

Above and below: Labels of typical Franco-American food products. Opposite: Campbell's Vegetable Soup advertisement, 1931.

Franco-American merged with Joseph Campbell Company, and though at least one of its products, Spaghetti à la Milanaise, continued to be manufactured, the company disappeared as a separate entity.

It is not entirely clear why Dorrance bought Franco-American. He certainly had faith in his own soups, which were outselling Franco-American's twenty to one, and he was not interested in maintaining a wide line of prepared foods. Years before, he had pared Campbell's product list until it included only soup and Pork & Beans. In any event, the June 1921 purchase was only a preparation for a business deal that took place six months later.

At a meeting of the board of directors on December 5, 1921, the Joseph Campbell Company — which had operated under at least four different names since its incorporation in 1869 — was formally dissolved. For the "sum of one dollar, lawful money of the United States," Joseph Campbell transferred its "business, property and assets" to a newly formed company.

By forming this new company, John Dorrance, the man in love with soup, had achieved his goal. He had created the largest and most profitable soup company in the United States and probably the world. Though it manufactured Pork & Beans and Franco-American spaghetti, it was only fitting, Dorrance thought, that its name reflect its most famous and profitable product. Dorrance did not call this new enterprise the Campbell *Food* Company. He named it the Campbell *Soup* Company.

It's not "vegetables" to them ... it's just good soup!

And without realizing it, they are eating 15 nourishing, health-giving vegetables!

"My, but I do wish those children would eat their vegetables. It's enough to drive me distracted—the trouble I have every day to coax them into eating vegetables."

Practically every mother has this same story to tell unless she gives the youngsters Campbell's Vegetable Soup. If your children are sulky and balky about eating these foods which they need so much for their proper growth and health, just place a bowlful of Campbell's Vegetable Soup in front of them. Watch it disappear!

Soup is an ideal way to eat vegetables because it retains their health-giving mineral salts in such rich abundance.

Vegetables served in other ways than in soup are apt to lose a valuable amount of their mineral salts which the cooking water absorbs.

In the Campbell's kitchens, the vegetables are cooked in their own essences and juices; all of this body-building goodness is in the soup, enriching it and making it especially wholesome for growing children. Give your children the real, sound benefits of Campbell's Vegetable Soup.

Your choice

Asparagus	Mock Turtle
Bean	Mulligatawny
Beef	Mutton
Bouillon	Ox Tail
Celery	Pea
Chicken	Pepper Pot
Chicken-Gumbo	Printanier
Clam Chowder	Tomato
Consomme	Vegetable
Julienne	Vegetable-Beef
Vermicelli-Tomato	

Home's the sweetest place on earth
  And victory is dearer,
For knowing, at each mighty stroke,
  That Campbell's Soup is nearer!

LOOK FOR THE RED-AND-WHITE LABEL

We Blend the Best

Beginning in late summer and continuing through the end of October, a line of trucks and farm wagons, sometimes nine miles long, began forming before daybreak along Second Street in Camden. It was tomato season, the time when this relatively fragile vegetable was ripe and thus ready to be made into Tomato Soup, the best selling of all Campbell products. The streets of Camden literally turned red from stray tomatoes falling from trucks. Each of these vehicles was loaded with between three and four tons of tomatoes — and not just any tomatoes, for the drivers hauling this produce from their south Jersey farms operated under contract to the Campbell Soup Company. For soup-making purposes, these were the best tomatoes that money could buy.

For such a common and popular vegetable, the tomato has a peculiar botanical background. Though universally grown and eaten as if it were a vegetable, no different than a cabbage or carrot, botanically the tomato is classified as a fruit. Like an apple's, its seeds are its means of reproduction. To be even more precise, the tomato is a berry since, like a strawberry, its many seeds, lacking stones, are scattered and embedded in its pulp. For purposes of trade, however, the tomato is a vegetable, having been so designated by an 1893 United States Supreme Court decision. Tomatoes, the court held, are "usually served at dinner in, with, or after the soup, fish, or meat, which constitute the principal part of the repast, and not, like fruits, generally as dessert," and thus they were subject to the usual duties levied on imported vegetables.

The tomato's history is equally surprising. According to legend, it was first discovered by Europeans shortly after Cortés landed in Mexico in 1519. A Jesuit priest accompanying him, the story continues, sent some seeds to his brother in Tangier, who planted and harvested the first tomatoes grown outside of the New World. How the cultivation of tomatoes traveled across the Mediterranean is an agricultural mystery, but by the end of the sixteenth century they were being grown in many European gardens, most often, it appears, as decorative plants. Though tomatoes had the reputation of being poisonous, by the mid-1700s they were sometimes eaten, most notably in Italy, where they were called *pomi d'oro*, or golden apples.

As was the case with many other culinary firsts, it was Thomas Jefferson

who introduced the tomato to the United States. But Jefferson was not immediately successful in his attempt to convince Americans of the value of the fruit, and well into the nineteenth century many people would have nothing to do with it. Some, however, tried to advance Jefferson's cause. One of these tomato lovers, a Salem, New Jersey, man named Robert Gibbon Johnson, is reported to have stood on the steps of the town courthouse and announced that he would, in full public view, consume an entire tomato, which he did, apparently with no dire consequences. Though his audience was impressed, it apparently did not follow Johnson's example.

Despite its lingering bad reputation, by the late nineteenth century the

---
◆◆◆

Opposite: Campbell workers sorting and culling fresh tomatoes, c. 1930. Below: Campbell's Tomato Soup fan used as a promotion in Canada, c. 1930.

---

tomato was slowly beginning to gain favor, occasionally being touted by physicians for its nutritional value. It even gained a certain cachet among the sophisticated and well-to-do, one commentator reporting that tomatoes were "served by everybody who has not deliberately made up his mind to be ranked among the nobodies." Thus, by the time Dr. Dorrance began manufacturing soups, the public's suspicions about this vegetable had been almost completely allayed, so much so that Tomato Soup quickly became the most popular of Campbell's original twenty-one kinds.

The tomato is a fairly difficult plant to grow well, particularly for soup-making purposes. Its ratio of acid to sugar must be well balanced, and since its pulp is used along with its juice, a good tomato must have thick, firm side walls. Even the shape is important: the deeper and more fully rounded the tomato, the more pulp there is below the less flavorful stem area. Finally, the color is crucial. A purplish hue fades under heat, and a light red leaves the soup looking weak and watery. The prime soup-making tomato is deep, vivid red.

Dorrance had always experimented with tomato cultivation at his Cinnaminson farm, but in 1912 he hired Harry Hall, an agricultural expert who was to become one of the world's leading authorities on the propagation and cultivation of tomatoes. Hall's official title was Superintendent of Campbell's Soup Farms, and his major responsibility was to advise farmers under contract to the company on all aspects of vegetable growing. As it had since it first began manufactur-

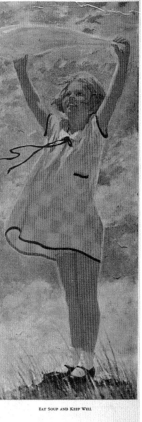

ing soup, Campbell took the quality of its ingredients very seriously, arguing that well-made soup was as fine a dish as any, not a hodgepodge of meats and vegetables rescued from the scrap heap. It was the job of Campbell agriculturalists to maintain the high quality of the vegetables used. As Hall once explained:

A large amount of the vegetables used by us are grown at Campbell's Soup Farms and by farmers located at nearby points. In this work we aim to contract with the most skillful and successful farmers who take a pride in their products and are therefore very keen to supply us with vegetables of the highest quality. One or more meetings are held each year, usually at Campbell's Soup Farms, where prominent speakers discuss the most approved methods of crop production. At these meetings liberal prizes are awarded for the best baskets of tomatoes, thus providing the opportunity to impress upon them our standards of perfection.

During the growing season Campbell contracted with about two thousand farmers to provide it with vegetables. Most of these farms were located in southern New Jersey relatively near Camden and, thus, a saving in trucking costs. (Hall described New Jersey as "the land of the good red tomato.") Farmers who grew vegetables such as carrots, peas, or beans were given all sorts of agricultural advice, but the tomato farmers received the greatest attention. They were actually provided with seeds, the product of Hall's time-consuming efforts to breed the perfect soup-making tomato.

Breeding tomatoes, as Hall once explained, takes a light, patient touch:

Above: Campbell's Tomato Soup advertisements, 1935. Opposite: Campbell's Cream of Mushroom Soup advertisement, 1934.

HOSTESSES UNAFRAID!

There's no "zero hour" for the hostess who approaches the dinner with every detail "just so". When her guests are assembled at her gleaming table and the soup is served, not so much as a flutter is noted in her demeanor. She has seen to that—beforehand.

The social test for a soup is a mighty good guide. Then, if ever, all criticism must be forestalled. And like the presiding lady herself, Campbell's Soups approach the critical moment "unafraid".

Skilled soup chefs of international training and reputation surely are a safe reliance when you entertain. And Campbell's chefs enjoy this special distinction.

Cream of Mushroom—that soup de luxe—comes from their hands in unexcelled and sumptuous richness. Yet it is but one of many Campbell's Soups that are at your instant disposal—fully equal to any occasion. Soups that sum up and combine countless home recipes and home "secrets" and home skills, as adapted and developed and perfected by professional soup specialists in Campbell's kitchens.

Double rich! Double strength!

Campbell's Soups bring you condensed, concentrated goodness. So when you add an equal quantity of water in your kitchen, you obtain twice the quantity of soup at no extra cost.

Campbells'

CREAM of MUSHROOM

LOOK FOR THE
RED-AND-WHITE LABEL

Health
is his middle name!

AND Campbell's Tomato Soup is one of his "pals"... they just naturally go together... the boy with his wide-awake appetite... the soup with its bright, enticing flavor and sunny wholesomeness... Notice how eagerly he enjoys its red-ripe tomato tang... Watch how promptly the soup disappears from his plate! ... And what a satisfaction it is to you to know that Campbell's make it with a care and skill just like your own... true home-made goodness for the family's benefit, but with much less effort by you... equally easy to serve as Tomato Soup (with water added) or Cream of Tomato (with milk added).

LOOK FOR THE
RED-AND-WHITE LABEL

With Campbell's Soup
To make me gay,
It's sure to be
My lucky day!

Campbell's Soups invite you
to "HOLLYWOOD HOTEL!"

A full-hour dramatic musical revue starring Dick Powell with famous radio and moving picture stars, Raymond Paige's Orchestra and the Hollywood Singers

Columbia Coast-to-Coast Network—Fridays—9 to 10 P. M.—(E.D.S.T.)

Campbell's Tomato Soup

Above: Campbell's Tomato Soup
advertisement, 1935.

It is necessary that the tomato flower's stamens or male organs be removed before the germs or polled grains have thoroughly ripened and are ready for distribution. This work is done at least twenty-four hours before the flower opens, the operation being performed by the use of small pointed pliers, care being taken that the other parts of the flower are not injured. In twenty-four to forty-eight hours after this work has been done, the pistil will be ripe to receive the pollen, which has been taken from a selected plant chosen as the male parent for the desired cross. If the work has been done properly, the small tomato begins its life of development, producing seeds which are to develop into new forms and from which we may be able to select a variety superior to either parent.

A steady hand is not all that is needed, however; this process must be repeated nine or ten times before a new breed of tomato is created. (Each generation is given an "F" number, representing in Mendelian terms a "filial generation.") At the time Hall began his work there were many varieties of commercial tomatoes: the Marglobe, the Greater Baltimore, the Pritchard, and the JTD, which he had named after his boss, John Thompson Dorrance. Later there was the Rutgers, which Hall, in association with the New Jersey Agriculture Station, created by crossing the Marglobe with the JTD. (The Marglobe was a fairly disease-resistant variety, but it was an "exterior ripener." When it looked ready for picking, its pulp was often still immature. The JTD, on the other hand, was an "interior ripener," and its color was good, but it was fairly vulnerable to disease. The Rutgers combined the best of these traits.)

At first Campbell provided seeds only to its contract farmers, but in 1918 a member of Hall's staff, named R. Vincent Crine, came up with a great idea: the tomato season could be extended if seeds were planted in the warm Georgia climate in January and February and the plants produced from them were shipped back to New Jersey when the weather permitted. This idea proved so workable that soon forty to fifty million seedlings were being grown each year, and each summer Campbell was assured a sufficient quantity of perfect, ripe tomatoes.

The only trouble with this abundance was that, unlike many other vegetables, the tomato, once it has ripened, has a relatively short shelf life. To produce the highest quality tomato soup it was necessary to process the tomato as soon after harvesting as possible. Since Tomato Soup was Campbell's largest-selling product, this meant that during tomato season the company had to forego the making of all other soups and concentrate solely on Tomato. In fact, early in the

1920s Campbell found it necessary to construct a new plant on the Camden waterfront designed primarily for the processing of tomato pulp. This factory, Plant No. 2, which later was equipped also to manufacture Pork & Beans and Tomato Juice, was once called "unquestionably the greatest industrial canning plant in the world."

The process of turning raw tomatoes into soup began each morning at 5:45, when the first farmer drove his load up to the loading dock where Campbell inspectors were waiting to grade the tomatoes. If they were good

Below: A towering conveyor line in Campbell's Camden factory carried tomatoes from the receiving and grading area to processing stations.

in color ("stylish," as Hall termed it) and free of growth cracks, mold, decay, and "cat faces" (hard black areas at the blossom end), they were graded "No. 1." For "No. 2s," which missed this mark because between 10 and 20 percent had disfigurements, the farmer was paid much less, since Campbell would have to throw away much of the load.

From the grading platforms the tomatoes were lifted in baskets on hangers into the factory, where they underwent a series of three washings before being placed on a conveyor belt that passed through the inspection station. There women discarded the bad or green tomatoes and trimmed those with flaws. The tomatoes were then ready for processing.

At this point they were fed into a hammer mill, a large machine with two sets of interlocking fingers. The raw pulp produced by this crusher, still containing seeds, was then piped to another floor of the factory and into one of fourteen 600-gallon steam-jacketed copper breaker kettles, in which it was simmered. To keep the pulp in suspension, each kettle was manned by a single worker who stirred it with a huge wooden paddle.

Once the pulp was cooked, it was emptied through a spout, piped to yet another floor, and fed into a series of three "Cyclones," machines with spinning blades that forced the pulp through fine-mesh screens, separating it from skin and seeds. (Dorrance's manufacturing instructions specified the exact size of the sieve in each Cyclone as well as the revolutions per minute most appropriate to each machine.) The resulting thick liquid was then loaded into trucks with stainless-steel tanks and transported to the soup-making building, where butter, herbs, spices, and other ingredients were blended with it in 110-gallon kettles made of solid Austrian nickel. The industrial cooking process was, if anything, even more carefully orchestrated than the making of the pulp:

The celery seed, cloves, allspice, bay leaves are weighed out according to above amounts or multiples thereof, then they are covered with cold water in a jacketed kettle and allowed to boil about ten minutes. This liquid is then drawn off from the kettle and passed through three thicknesses of cheesecloth, which should be allowed to stand several hours before using. The salt, red and white pepper are weighed out and placed in one tin vessel and thoroughly mixed. The reason for this mixing is that it keeps the pepper from forming lumps in the kettle. The onions and garlic are run through the Enterprise cutter.

Sugar and butter are placed in separate tin receptacles. The required amount of flour is placed in a mixer, and to this is added uncooked tomato pulp in such a quantity that, when it is mixed together, it forms a thick paste. The tomato product sent to the

"Guess what I want for lunch!"

Her eagerness for Campbell's Vegetable Soup shows what a healthy, wholesome, normal appetite she has. Boys and girls are naturally fond of this famous soup because it tastes so mighty good and because it is real, substantial food—just the kind that quiets the steady, gnawing hunger of the active child.

Every spoonful is laden with the finest garden vegetables cooked in rich beef broth to save their healthful goodness in full strength. It's all in the soup—to delight your children's taste and benefit them regularly and often. And it's made in the world's greatest soup-kitchens—universally trusted for strict purity and quality.

LOOK FOR THE
RED-AND-WHITE LABEL

EAT SOUP
AND KEEP WELL

Mother's willing
Helpers we—
Campbell's Soups
And busy Me!

21 kinds to choose from . .

Asparagus	Mulligatawny
Bean	Mutton
Beef	Ox Tail
Bouillon	Pea
Celery	Pepper Pot
Chicken	Printanier
Chicken-Gumbo	Tomato
Clam Chowder	Tomato-Okra
Consommé	Vegetable
Julienne	Vegetable-Beef
Mock Turtle	Vermicelli-Tomato

10 cents a can

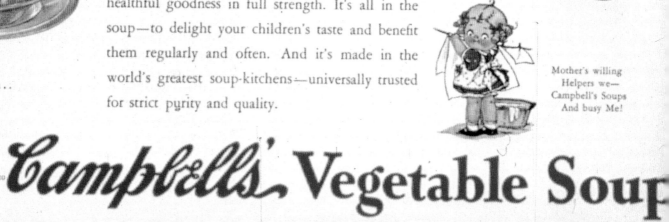

Campbell's Vegetable Soup

The Dorrance Family Tree

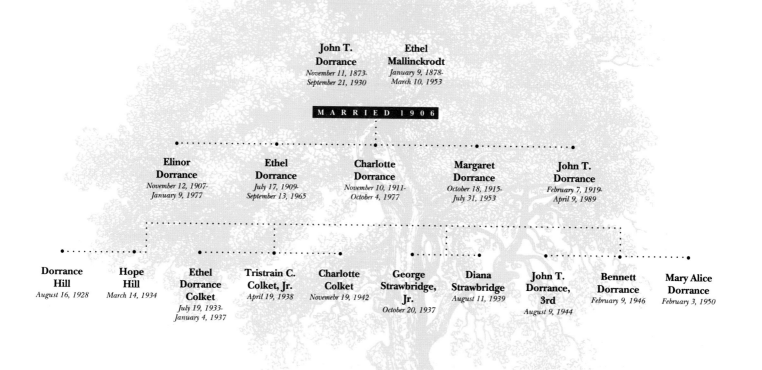

John T. Dorrance
November 11, 1873-
September 21, 1930

Ethel Mallinckrodt
January 9, 1878-
March 10, 1953

MARRIED 1906

Elinor Dorrance
November 12, 1907-
January 9, 1977

Ethel Dorrance
July 17, 1909-
September 13, 1965

Charlotte Dorrance
November 10, 1911-
October 4, 1977

Margaret Dorrance
October 18, 1915-
July 31, 1953

John T. Dorrance
February 7, 1919-
April 9, 1989

Dorrance Hill
August 16, 1928

Hope Hill
March 14, 1934

Ethel Dorrance Colket
July 19, 1933-
January 4, 1937

Tristrain C. Colket, Jr.
April 19, 1938

Charlotte Colket
Novemebr 19, 1942

George Strawbridge, Jr.
October 20, 1937

Diana Strawbridge
August 11, 1939

John T. Dorrance, 3rd
August 9, 1944

Bennett Dorrance
February 9, 1946

Mary Alice Dorrance
February 3, 1950

soup department is run into kettles, and the kettles are filled up from time to time with raw pulp so that, at the end of the cooking, each kettle contains 95 gallons.

The nutcoa or salad oil which we use should be placed in the tomato pulp before cooking. This will keep the kettles from boiling over, hence its use. The onions and garlic should be placed in the kettle at the same time. The flour paste above spoken of is added and the soup constantly stirred. The liquid spices should then be added as well as pepper, salt, sugar, and Worcester sauce. The soup is now boiled for about two or three minutes, just long enough to cause the flour to thicken. The soup is then drawn off and passed through a Cyclone containing a #16 iron sieve, paddles without brushes running about 250 r.p.m. From this Cyclone it is passed into a

machine containing a brass wire screen, 22 holes to the inch, in order to allow any black specks or other material, which might possibly be in the soup, to get out.

When the Tomato Soup was cooked to the satisfaction of an attending chef who stood by stirring and tasting, it was then piped to the factory's canning section. After the cans were filled and sealed, they were placed in baskets and loaded into a retort, a tall, cylindrical steam cooker. When the proper processing time had passed (about thirty minutes) the cans were lifted out, cooled (by spraying them with water), and taken to another section of the factory, where the familiar red-and-white Campbell's Soup labels were affixed.

By the mid-1920s, despite a slight downturn during World War I, soup cans rolled off the assembly line by the millions (ten million a day during tomato season). This, of course, translated into a significant yearly growth in sales. In 1918 alone the company showed a 24-percent increase in sales, and less than ten years later, in 1927, it grossed $50 million. Demand for Campbell's Soups was so huge that even additions to the Camden factory could not keep up, so in 1930 an $8-million-dollar plant was built in Chicago.

All of these plants and properties, along with the other assets of the Campbell Soup Company, were owned by a single man, Dr. John Thompson Dorrance. As a privately held corporation, Campbell was not obliged to open its books, but industry analysts estimated that it made approximately 6/10 of a cent profit on each can sold. Given the fact that by the late twenties it was packing approximately a billion cans per year, the company probably was turning a $6-million profit.

Though the Campbell Soup Company had made Dorrance a rich man, he did not spend ostentatiously. He apparently had only two real interests in life: his family and his company. He maintained Woodcrest, his Radnor mansion, at a cost of $100,000 a year. Family vacations in the summer were spent in Bar Harbor, Maine, where he rented either Briar Cliff from Mrs. Edward B. McLean or Missentop from Henry Morgenthau. In Maine large parties were thrown for his daughters, as they were in Philadelphia, where three floors of the Bellevue-Stratford Hotel were dec-

orated with exotic plants and flowers and cages of tropical birds.

Other than on his family, however, Dorrance hardly spent a dime. He did fish in Montana, belong to various clubs, and serve on the boards of some large corporations, but for the most part he simply worked. Even after moving his family to Main Line Philadelphia, he kept the Cinnaminson farm open, and it was there on September 21, 1930, at the age of fifty-six, that he died.

For the previous thirty-three years Dorrance had labored daily, sometimes almost single-handedly, in the pursuit of his main goal in life: to make his firm the best and most prosperous soup company in the world. (By "best" he meant that it manufactured products vastly superior to any others on the market.) The effort to drive a machine of such perfection and proportion, like any single-minded ambition, was both Herculean and exhausting. Dorrance succeeded by pure assertion; he charged himself and others with this task and refused to accept failure. At the end of his life friends and associates thought he looked weary and careworn, which he probably was, but he had fulfilled his chief goals and ensured the well-being of his family and of his company.

At the time of his death Dorrance's personal net worth was approximately $115 million, which made him, after Payne Whitney and Thomas Fortune Ryan, the third richest man in the United States. All of this money was left to his family. The provisions of the will were fairly simple. After inheritance taxes were paid, the estate was to be divided into eight equal parts: two each

Above: Arthur Calbraith Dorrance, who became president of Campbell Soup Company following the death of his brother John on September 21, 1930.

"No one has to tell me it's Campbell's"

NO, there's no mistaking Campbell's Tomato Juice . . . once you've tasted its true, tangy tomato flavor. Your first taste will convince you of that . . . so why put off that delightful experience a single day?

The new large size . . . 10c a 14-oz. can.

Campbell's TOMATO JUICE

LOOK FOR THE RED-AND-WHITE LABEL

Yes··· and he likes this soup, too!

21 kinds to choose from...

Asparagus
Beef
Bouillon
Celery
Chicken
Chicken-Gumbo
Clam Chowder
Consommé
Julienne
Mock Turtle
Mushroom (Cream of)
Mutton
Noodle with chicken
Ox Tail
Pea
Pepper Pot
Printanier
Tomato
Vegetable
Vegetable-Beef

LOOK FOR THE RED-AND-WHITE LABEL

Double rich! Double strength!
Campbell's Soups bring you condensed, concentrated goodness. You are buying double richness—double strength. So when you add an equal quantity of water to your kitchen, you obtain twice the quantity of soup at no extra cost.

Hours of play in the glowing sunshine...racing at topmost speed in the open air...pausing to pick the flowers to be carried proudly away...then homeward bound with the trophies of the field and an appetite that only lusty food will answer.

Delight and satisfy the children's hunger with Campbell's Vegetable Soup. Each spoonful of it is laden with substantial goodness.

Its fresh, wholesome, right-out-of-the-garden flavor instantly appeals to the alert, youthful taste. And as the youngsters enjoy this soup, they are getting the full benefit of 15 choice vegetables, cooked in rich, invigorating beef broth. Exactly what growing young bodies require.

Made by Campbell's! This means that the soup has been made with the strict care and attention to detail that you would give in your own kitchen.

Campbell's Vegetable Soup
CONTAINING RICH BEEF BROTH PLUS 15 GARDEN VEGETABLES

"*Can't waste a drop!*"

He isn't going to miss any of it — not he! It tastes too good...so up goes the edge of the bowl...determined clicks of the spoon...and mother makes a mental note to give him Campbell's Vegetable Soup often!

Lucky decision, both for him and for her...since this soup just teems with vegetables...he gets the full benefit of their right-out-of-the-garden goodness...and she has an ideal answer to one of her child-feeding problems — vegetables in a form he always likes.

Especially is she gratified to know that Campbell's make their soups with such infinite care and patience ...such minute attention to all the niceties of the kitchen... why, even she could not be more particular!

Double rich! Double strength!
Campbell's Soups are made as in your own home kitchen, except that the broth is double strength. So when you add an equal quantity of water, you obtain twice as much full-flavored soup at no extra cost.

21 kinds to choose from...

Asparagus
Beef
Bouillon
Celery
Chicken
Chicken-Gumbo
Clam Chowder
Consommé
Julienne
Mock Turtle
Mulligatawny
Mushroom (Cream of)
Mutton
Noodle with chicken
Ox Tail
Pea
Pepper Pot
Printanier
Tomato
Vegetable
Vegetable-Beef

LOOK FOR THE RED-AND-WHITE LABEL

Campbell's Soups forever,
And our colors, Red-and-White—
They give us vim and vigor
To take the field and fight!

Campbell's Vegetable Soup
CONTAINING RICH BEEF BROTH PLUS 15 GARDEN VEGETABLES

Reprinted from January, 1935, Woman's Home Companion

Opposite: Campbell's Tomato Juice advertisement from 1934. Above: These Campbell's Vegetable Soup advertisements from 1935 (right) and 1936 focused, like so many others, on the feeding of children.

to his wife and son, one to each of his four daughters. Ownership of the Campbell Soup Company resided in the estate, which, the will stated, was forbidden from interfering with the declaration of dividends.

After Dorrance's death his brother Arthur Calbraith Dorrance, who had joined the company in 1920 and risen through the ranks to become vice president, was appointed president. Like John, Arthur made the company his sole and abiding interest. Also like his brother, he was a shrewd businessman, which he needed to be since the Great Depression began shortly after he took control of the company. Times were hard, and even products as inexpensive and popular as Campbell's Soup suffered. In 1932, for instance, sales dropped 23 percent from the previous year.

Campbell also, for the first time, faced competition in the field of condensed soup. In the mid-thirties Albanus Phillips, head of the Maryland-based Phillips Food Company, began marketing fifteen varieties of condensed soup, seven of which he sold for five cents a can. (Campbell spent more than the wholesale price of Phillips's soups on ingredients alone.) But Arthur Dorrance did not lower prices, nor did he reduce quality. He was sufficiently confident to let consumers choose, which they did, and Phillips's foray into the condensed-soup business was short-lived. Dorrance also did not budge when faced with the threat of Heinz and Hormel, both of which were manufacturing more expensive ready-to-serve soups. He believed that customers would stick with Campbell, and they did.

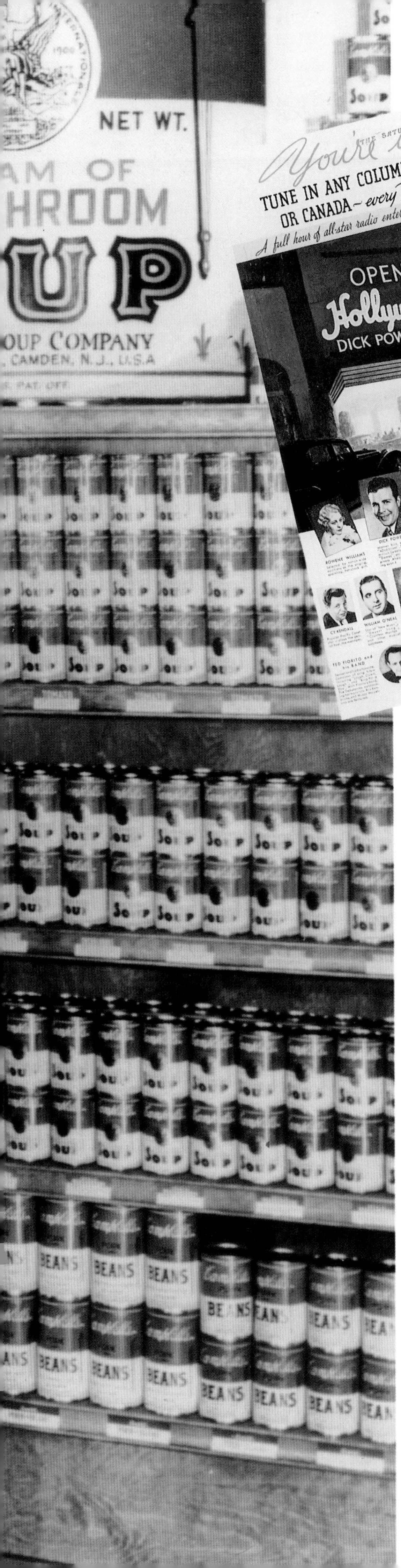

Net WT.
...AM OF
...HROOM
...UP
...OUP COMPANY
CAMDEN, N.J., U.S.A
PAT. OFF.

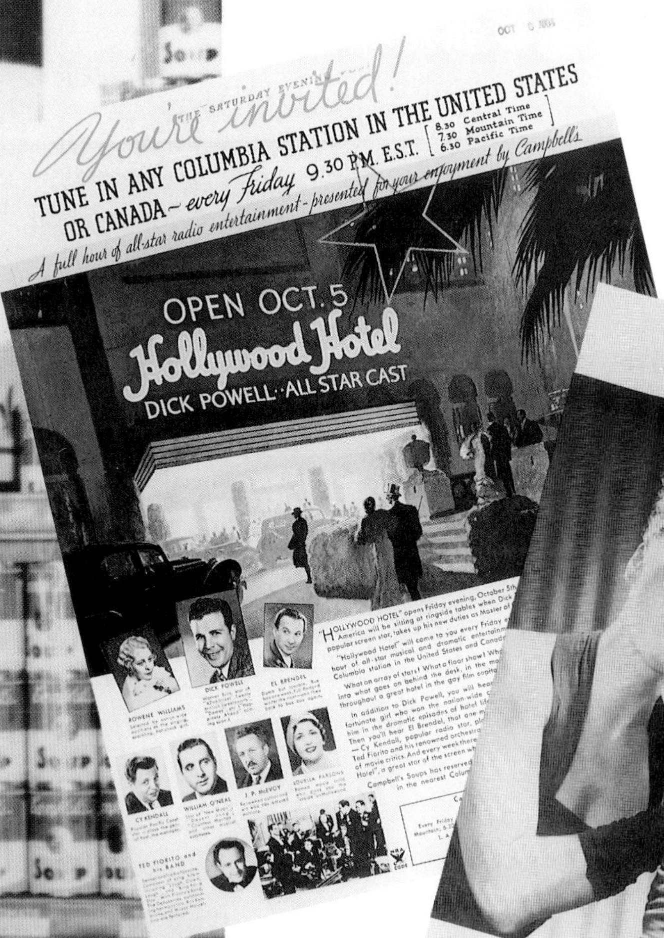

You're invited!

THE SATURDAY EVENING...

TUNE IN ANY COLUMBIA STATION IN THE UNITED STATES
OR CANADA — *every Friday* 9.30 P.M. E.S.T.

| 8.30 Central Time |
| 7.30 Mountain Time |
| 6.30 Pacific Time |

A full hour of all-star radio entertainment - presented for your enjoyment by Campbell's

OPEN OCT. 5
Hollywood Hotel
DICK POWELL · ALL STAR CAST

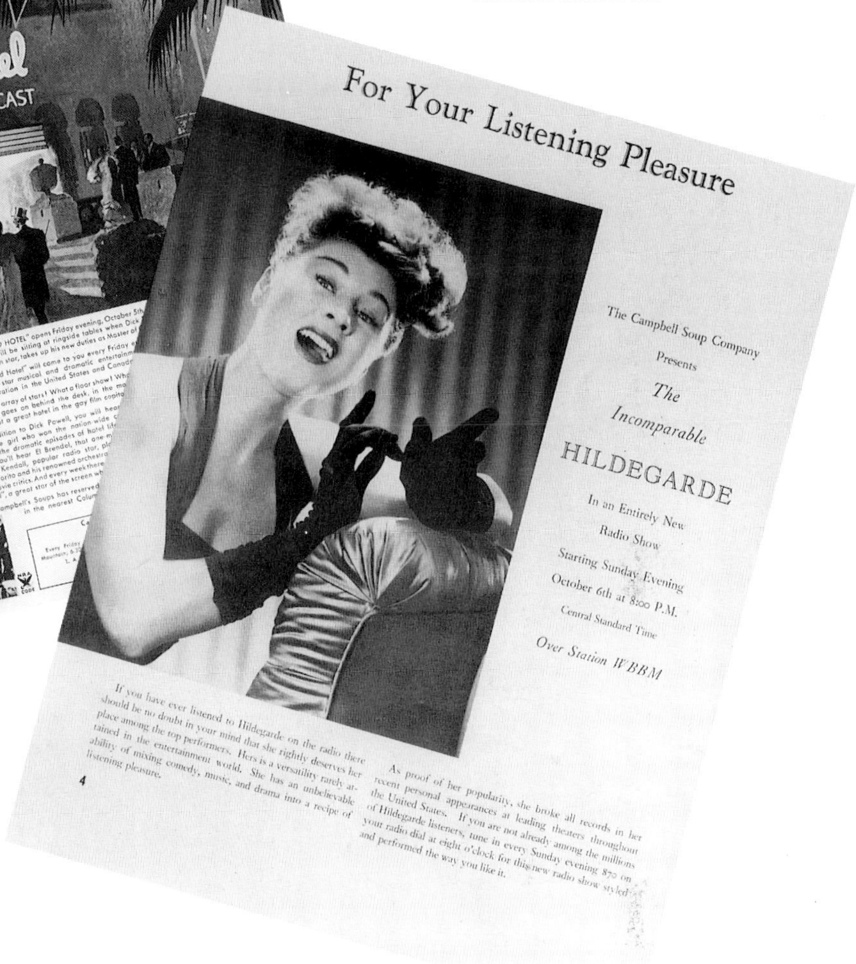

For Your Listening Pleasure

The Campbell Soup Company
Presents
The
Incomparable
HILDEGARDE
In an Entirely New
Radio Show
Starting Sunday Evening
October 6th at 8:00 P.M.
Central Standard Time
Over Station WBBM

Dorrance did, however, slightly modify the company's advertising policy. The first change, which had been underway since 1922, involved the Campbell Kids. The Kids had always played a curious role in the company's advertising. Without doubt, cuteness and whimsy had widespread appeal, especially to the mothers and children Campbell was seeking to attract. At the same time, though, there was a serious side to soup, represented by publications like *Campbell's Menu Book* and *Helps for the Hostess*. Indeed, the Campbell Kids drawings in the latter do seem a little out of place. As Leonard Frailey, secretary of the

Joseph Campbell Company wrote in 1912, "Because it has been said that one's business should not be turned into a jest, some people have been disposed to think we are building the wrong foundation using these semi-grotesque little creatures as trade figures."

But Campbell kept the Kids, arguing that they gave an "atmosphere of buoyant health and happiness to every Campbell's Soup ad," and until 1921 they appeared in every one of the company's advertisements. Through the twenties and thirties,

Below: Campbell's Consommé advertisement, 1935. Opposite: Advertisement for five of Campbell's most exotic and difficult-to-prepare soups, 1933.

however, the Kids began to be de-emphasized, both in the number of ads in which they appeared and in their prominence on the page. (By 1937 the Kids appeared in only about a third of Campbell's ads.) In 1937 the advertising magazine *Printer's Ink* described their old and new roles:

The Campbell Kids gave the advertising certain qualities of good cheer, friendliness and informality which placed it in market contrast to the somber King Kong qualities and sophomoric intensity of some modern food advertising. But the Campbell Kids are not the prominent personalities they once were. They still appear, but you don't see them at the top of the page much. Their fade-out doesn't mean a change of view, however — ads go on in various ways appealing to children and mothers. Today children in Campbell ads are more realistic.

One of the reasons for this change was the Depression. Like most other advertisers, Campbell sought to uplift customers by means of their advertising copy and illustrations. Frequently in its ads — many of which were drawn by famous illustrators such as Norman Rockwell and Jessie Willcox Smith — well-dressed families were depicted sitting around the dining-room table enjoying healthful bowls of soup. In others, astute and responsible house-wives were shown providing their families with economical yet good-tasting fare. In short, these advertise-ments approached a serious problem (the health and welfare of the American family during bad times) with a serious yet supportive message: Campbell's Soup is flavorful, nutri-tious, and above all, inexpensive.

The Campbell Kids also played a very diminished role on radio, the newest advertising medium. Some thought was originally given to provid-ing them with voices, but since they were being downplayed anyway, this idea apparently was dropped. Campbell's first foray into radio was the 1931 sponsorship of an early-morning jazz show featuring Andy Sanella. Campbell's advertising department was not satisfied with the results of this effort, and the sponsor-ship lasted only a year. In 1934 radio advertising was resumed when the company sponsored the variety show

LADIES' HOME JOURNAL

Consommé THAT JELLS *right in the can*

... on ice ..... in your refrigerator

HOW you will delight in Jellied Consommé, now that Campbell's make it so easy for you to serve it!... It's so cool and refreshing and sparkling... it's something so new and different for the warm weather meals... it has such a delicious and appealing flavor that the family will eagerly welcome it!

To many and many a woman, Jellied Consommé has been something wished for, seldom served, because making it would mean more tedious kitchen-work just when everyone wishes to escape it... Now Campbell's bring this hot-weather treat to the family table, with next to no home preparation at all.

All you have to do is place a can of Campbell's Consommé in the refrigerator for four hours... and out it comes, an amber-clear, delicious jellied soup ready to give its dainty sparkle and refreshment to any meal... And the flavor! ... Here is all the strength and richness of the finest beef broth, seasoned with the skill of the true expert... enticing to the taste... appetizing... a real help in making your summer table more attractive.

On the air!
"HOLLYWOOD HOTEL"
Starring DICK POWELL!
In a full hour dramatic musical scene with famous radio and moving picture stars, Raymond Paige's Orchestra and the Hollywood Singers.
C. B. S. Coast-to-Coast
Fridays—9 to 10 P. M.—(E. D. S. T.)

Campbell's

To serve JELLIED Place Campbell's Consommé can, before opening, on ice in refrigerator for four hours. Then open can and place jellied contents in cooled bouillon cups. Serve immediately.

To serve HOT To the contents of Campbell's Consommé can add one can of cold water, heat to boiling point and serve. Salt to taste.

LOOK FOR THE RED-AND-WHITE LABEL

CONSOMMÉ SOUP

CONSOMMÉ

Delicious and "unusual" soups

that are so difficult to make at home!

The sparkle of the sea!
Even if you dwell far inland, Campbell's world-renowned chefs make for you Clam Chowder that has the ocean's refreshing tang in its irresistible flavor.

EAT SOUP
AND KEEP WELL

There was a time when you had to visit the fashionable hotel restaurants and the smart cafés to get soups like these. Although your appetite longed for them because of their delightful contrast and novelty, you never used to have them at home—they are such troublesome soups to make.

Now, however, Campbell's famous chefs bring them to your table in all their perfection—requiring practically no work in your kitchen—yet adding so much to the goodness of your meals.

Only the greatest soup-kitchens in the world — Campbell's — could offer you such a complete and helpful variety in soups which are unequalled for their deliciousness!

Could you make it?
Real Philadelphia Pepper Pot! Campbell's blend it from an exclusive old Colonial recipe that brings you this famous soup just as the founders of the nation enjoyed it.

Chicken Soup of the Orient!
Campbell's Mulligatawny, with its curry and its East India chutney is a genuine "surprise" and pleasure.

A real change!
Campbell's Mock Turtle Soup—a hint from the gay cafés—a luscious temptation to a family appetite eager for something out of the ordinary. You'll want to serve it often.

A "find" for your table!
Campbell's Ox Tail Soup—so delightfully different, so richly satisfying that the whole family welcomes it.

Built upon
The modern plan,
I'm a big, strong
    Campbell's man!

21 kinds to choose from...

Asparagus	Mulligatawny
Bean	Mutton
Beef	Ox Tail
Bouillon	Pea
Celery	Printanier
Chicken	Pepper Pot
Chicken-Gumbo	Tomato
Clam Chowder	Tomato-Okra
Consommé	Vegetable
Julienne	Vegetable-Beef
Mock Turtle	Vermicelli-Tomato

10 cents a can

LOOK FOR THE
RED-AND-WHITE LABEL

EVERY KIND OF SOUP YOU EVER WANT—EACH SOUP A MASTERPIECE!

21 adventures in good eating

And what good eating it is! With a row of Campbell's Soups before you, the particular soup for the particular occasion suggests itself — and you know, beforehand, what a success it will be. So convenient, too — just glance at your Campbell's shelf, select the soup of the day, and it's ready almost while you're thinking about it.

ASPARAGUS
Purée of luscious asparagus. Strictly vegetable. Makes delightful Cream of Asparagus.

BEAN with bacon.
New! The "beani-est" soup you ever tasted. Plump whole beans in a thick bean purée deliciously flavored with bacon.

BEEF
A thick, hunger-satisfying soup containing hearty diced meat, vegetables and barley.

BOUILLON
A clear soup, made from choice beef, blended with herbs, vegetables and aromatic spices. Invigorating!

CELERY
Made from the choicest quality celery. Strictly vegetable. Delicious as a Cream of Celery.

CHICKEN
Not just a broth — it's the real Chicken Soup with tender pieces of chicken meat and rice.

CHICKEN-GUMBO
A famous Southern Creole chicken and vegetable style soup — flavored with okra and tomato. Unusual!

CLAM CHOWDER
All the broth and meat of juicy clams — flavored with tomatoes — and garnished with potatoes and onions.

CONSOMMÉ
The formal soup. Beautifully clear. A rich beef broth, lightly seasoned — and delicately flavored with vegetables.

MOCK TURTLE
Beef broth, tomatoes, celery, herbs, toothsome pieces of meat, richly blended with sherry.

MULLIGATAWNY
An unusual Oriental style chicken soup. Laden with flavorous vegetables, herbs and seasoning.

MUSHROOM (Cream of)
A purée made from choicest cultivated, whole, fresh mushrooms blended with fresh, double-thick cream — liberally garnished with mushrooms.

MUTTON
Mutton broth garnished with fresh mutton, barley and vegetables — splendid for children and invalids.

NOODLE with chicken
A full-bodied chicken broth containing hearty egg noodles and delicious pieces of tender chicken meat.

OX TAIL
Vegetables, barley and sliced ox tail joints in an Old English style ox tail broth — with sherry.

PEA
Purée of delicious, nourishing peas. Strictly vegetable. Even more nourishing served as Cream of Pea.

PEPPER POT
The real famous "Philadelphia Pepper Pot" with macaroni dumplings, potatoes, spicy seasoning and meat.

SCOTCH BROTH
A thick, substantial, hearty soup, delicious with meat and vegetables. A new soup — a different soup.

TOMATO
Pure tomato juices and luscious tomato "meat" in a sparkling purée enriched with finest creamery butter. Strictly vegetable. Serve it too as Cream of Tomato.

VEGETABLE
It's a meal in itself. 15 fine garden vegetables cooked in rich beef broth. A great family favorite everywhere.

VEGETABLE-BEEF
Real old-fashioned Vegetable Soup — rich beef broth, thick with vegetables and substantial pieces of meat.

"Hollywood Hotel." A year later this program was replaced by "The Burns and Allen Show," and in 1938 by the hugely popular "Amos 'n' Andy."

A slip of the tongue on "Amos 'n' Andy" actually affected the sales of what is now one of Campbell's most popular soups. In 1934 Campbell had introduced a new soup called Chicken with Noodles, which enjoyed only moderate success. The company thought it was a very good soup and could not understand why it was not more popular. After much discussion, it was decided that Chicken with Noodles would be one of the soups most prominently advertised on "Amos 'n' Andy." One night Freeman Gosden,

who played Amos, misread his copy and called the product Chicken Noodle Soup. Within days the company began receiving large orders for this new soup. For some reason the slight shift in nomenclature mattered, and within a very short time the soup was formally renamed Chicken Noodle.

For most of its early history, the company's list of soups remained remarkably stable. In 1916 Clam Bouillon was dropped, and in 1918 Vegetable Beef was added. (The creation of Vegetable Beef was the result of the demand during World War I for an especially nutritious soup for soldiers.) In the mid-thirties,

however, the manufacture of six of the original twenty-one soups was discontinued. Not surprisingly, these were, to the taste of the average American, some of the more exotic: Julienne, Printanier, Mulligatawny, Mutton, Tomato Okra, and Vermicelli-Tomato.

Taking the place of these soups were, among others, Chicken Noodle, Cream of Mushroom, Bean with Bacon, and Vegetarian. Of them, Cream of Mushroom was certainly the most significant in terms of the changing state of the Campbell company. Shortly after the introduction of the initial line of Campbell's condensed soups, it was suggested that, because of their extreme concentration, a single can of undiluted soup could double as a sauce or stock. "Many times," the booklet *Helps for the Hostess* stated, "unattractive left-overs are thrown away when, by using a can of Campbell's Soup, they could have been made into an attractive, appetizing dish." The booklet then gave what Escoffier would have termed the "culinary operation" to be followed:

The general rule for making Campbell's sauces is:

1 cup Campbell's Soup
1 tablespoon butter
1 tablespoon flour

Melt butter, add flour, blend, and pour in soup. Then add chopped leftovers and serve in one of various ways. Use on toast with rice; with pastry shell or vol-au-vent, or bake and scallop in oven for a few minutes; or pour over macaroni or noodles.

Campbell's Soup very much resembled Continental stocks and sauces, and the Joseph Campbell Company suggested their use as such. Why bother to make stock? *Helps for the Hostess* asked. "In any recipe where it says stock use a can of Campbell's Bouillon, Consommé, Julienne, or if you want small, dainty vegetables, Printanier." And what better base for a sauce than Tomato Soup? One could quickly make Spaghetti à la Campbell with just the following ingredients: "1 can Campbell's Tomato Soup; 1/2 lb. smallest tube spaghetti; 1/2 lb. sliced smoked ham; 1 can button mushrooms (or 1/2 lb. fresh); 2 small onions, thickly sliced; 3 small peppers, thinly

sliced; 1/2 tsp. thyme; 1 clove garlic; 2 tbs. olive oil; and grated cheese (American or Parmesan)."

This recipe is remarkable for a couple of reasons, the first being that spaghetti at the time was seldom served in the United States. Well into the 1950s spaghetti was an ethnic dish, prepared mostly by Italian immigrants for Italian immigrants. Then there were some of the other ingredients. At the time *Helps for the Hostess* was published (1916), olive oil and Parmesan cheese would have been difficult to find at the local grocery store, and garlic was hardly ever used by the average American housewife, and then only to rub the inside surface of a salad bowl. "Back then," Betty Fussel has written about the pre–World War II era, "to eat a loaf of garlic bread was an act of bravado and to eat a garlic-laden spaghetti sauce was an act of liberation."

During the first thirty years of its history, Campbell quite sparingly published recipes that used soup as a sauce, and when it did, Tomato Soup was usually called for. One of the most long lasting, though perhaps the oddest, was for Tomato Soup Cake; the ingredients were: "2 tbs. shortening; 1 c. sugar; 1 egg (well beaten); 1 can Campbell's Tomato Soup; 2 c. flour; 1 tsp. ground cloves; 1/2 tsp. mace; 1/2 tsp. nutmeg; 1/2 tsp. baking soda; and 1 c. seeded raisins." The use of soup as sauce took a huge leap forward, however, when Campbell introduced Cream of Mushroom Soup in 1934. Like Tomato, Cream of Mushroom was both an eating and cooking soup. More importantly, its use in sauces was easy for the American

•••

Opposite: When full production resumed after World War II, Campbell was able to advertise the availability of sufficient stocks of its twenty-one kinds of soup. Above: An ad of 1943 reiterated the convenience and cost savings for the busy housewife and mother in serving Campbell's soups.

—then back to school keen and alert

No "sleepyheads" for them at school after a tempting lunch of Campbell's Vegetable Soup. See them "go" for its fifteen different delicious vegetables, and the long-simmered beef stock. Here's a delightful meal in itself with plenty of body and substance to it, without being heavy. And that means mental alertness for the afternoon's work, with lots of energy for play after school's out.

Busy mothers will also appreciate this — Campbell's Vegetable Soup is ready to serve in just a few minutes. So why not have it often? Its fine home-like flavor appeals to the grown-ups, too.

Campbell's Vegetable Soup

CONTAINING 15 GARDEN VEGETABLES PLUS RICH BEEF STOCK

21 kinds to choose from . . . Asparagus, Bean with bacon, Beef, Bouillon, Celery, Chicken, Chicken Gumbo, Clam Chowder, Consommé, Consommé-Printanier, Mock Turtle, Mulligatawny, Cream of Mushroom, Noodle with chicken, Ox Tail, Pea, Pepper Pot, Scotch Broth, Tomato, Vegetable, Vegetable-Beef

Look for the Red-and-White Label

Above: Due to a wartime shortage of tin plate, Campbell manufactured its first dry soup mix, which it marketed under the Franco-American label. Opposite: Campbell's Vegetable Soup advertisement, 1937. Below: During the Second World War, as it had during the First World War, Campbell promoted its soups as nutritious, easy to prepare, and hearty.

housewife to understand. One of the most popular recipes was Cream of Mushroom Gravy, which used the soup as a thickener of sorts:

Add to the drippings of a roast beef one-half cupful of water, and scrape the brown from the sides of the pan. Add one can of Campbell's Cream of Mushroom Soup and stir until well blended and smooth. Bring to a boil and serve piping hot. It may be made thinner, if desired, by adding more water. This makes an excellent gravy for roast beef and is far superior to the usual brown gravy.

Housewives agreed that it did make an excellent gravy, and Cream of Mushroom became the first Campbell's

Soup to be widely used as a sauce. Until 1934, most Campbell's recipe books were not much more than ten to fifteen pages long and contained about a dozen recipes. By 1941, when Campbell published its first full-length cookbook, *Easy Ways to Good Meals*, the idea of soup as sauce was starting to take hold of the American housewife's imagination. This shift in the use of soup turned out to be one of the most consequential in the company's history, the sales of cooking soups such as Cream of Mushroom eventually growing to around 30 percent of the company's business.

Despite these changes in the Campbell Soup line, the company still limited the number of soups manufactured to twenty-one. The mystique of this tradition was broken when William Beverly Murphy, a young, newly hired executive asked Arthur Dorrance if there was anything sacred about that number. In his hometown of Appleton,

Wisconsin, Murphy said, some cookbooks listed two hundred or more soups: Cream of Potato, Cream of Spinach, Cream of Chicken, Canadian Style Pea Soup. Dorrance was interested. The salesmen will raise a ruckus, he replied, but let's go ahead.

Murphy, who had been trained as a chemical engineer, had come to Campbell from the A. C. Nielsen Company, where he had been primarily responsible for the creation of the Nielsen Food Index. Arthur Dorrance, who subscribed to the Nielsen service, had met Murphy and, thinking that

he would have a fine future with Campbell, offered him a job as assistant general sales manager in 1938. Murphy, who wanted to be more of a generalist in business, at first turned Dorrance down, but later that year, when Dorrance approached him again, this time offering him the job of assistant to the president in charge of finding ways of expanding the business, Murphy accepted.

Shortly thereafter the United States entered World War II. Murphy left to join the War Production Board in Washington, where he worked on the development of the B-29 bomber. The Campbell Soup Company itself participated in the war effort, manufacturing special canned products for the army and navy. In addition the company, following federal wartime regulations covering the use of packaging materials and in particular scarce tin plate, was forced to cut back production. Despite shortages Campbell did manage to introduce a few new products. In 1941 it offered Franco-American Macaroni for the first time, and in 1943 the company introduced its first dry soup, under the Franco-American label. (Not satisfied with the packaging, Campbell withdrew the dry soups a year later.)

After the war, with the gradual lifting of most restrictions, Campbell resumed full production. Having survived the Depression and World War II, the company looked forward to an era of increased prosperity. Unfortunately, less than a year after the war ended, Arthur Dorrance, then fifty-three years old, died suddenly on September 21, 1946. Coincidentally, he died on the same day of the month

Many a soldier on field duty tucks his can of army rations under the motor hood of his jeep. When mealtime rolls around, there is his chow, warm and ready for roadside eating.

HOW TO PULL A HOT DINNER OUT OF A JEEP

IT'S JUST ANOTHER example of good old American ingenuity. But it enables the men of our Armed Forces, even when many miles from their base, to eat good American food, cooked the way a man enjoys it.

Packers of canned foods are playing a vital part in the feeding of our overseas men. The makers of Campbell's Soups, for instance, devote an important part of their production to the making and canning of balanced meat-and-vegetable dishes, developed by Army Quartermaster experts, for far-off battlefront eating. Millions of cans of these field rations are made in Campbell's kitchens . . . a part of the all-important job of keeping a great army well nourished at all times.

Our war-busy people on the home front, too, need the sort of meals that keep folks going. A family lunch or supper built around Campbell's Soup is a meal that's satisfying in deep, full flavor and in good, hearty nourishment. And, easy to fix, these soups fit well into the planning of wartime meals.

The makers of Campbell's Soups are proud to do their part, along with others of the canning industry, in feeding our fighting men as well as their families at home.

★ ★ ★

Army field rations, cooked in the U.S.A., go to our fighting men packed in cans. So if tin cans are collected in your locality, salvage every can you open. Fold in both ends, remove label, wash and flatten. Tin is vital to the war!

CAMPBELL SOUP COMPANY
MAKERS OF FOODS FOR VICTORY

Above and right: Campbell manufactured some food for the military with the help of off-duty service personnel. In 1943 these sailors helped out Campbell in packing a tomato crop threatened with spoiling.

RR TYPE RATION
MEAT & VEGETABLE HASH
NET WEIGHT 12 OZ.

Ingredients: Beef, water, pork, potatoes, onions, salt, celery salt, and spice.

U. S. INSPECTED AND PASSED BY DEPARTMENT OF AGRICULTURE EST. 4

PACKED BY
CAMPBELL SOUP COMPANY
CAMDEN, N. J., U. S. A.

that his brother John had died. John Thompson Dorrance, Jr., Dr. Dorrance's only son, was at the time only twenty-five years old and thus unprepared to take over the company. W. B. Murphy, then executive vice president, whom Arthur Dorrance had been grooming to replace him, was also thought to be too young to be named president. The board appointed James McGowan, who had been with the company since 1908, president, the first non-Dorrance to run the company since Arthur Dorrance the elder had purchased the company in 1893.

The Campbell Soup Company was about to enter its second great period of expansion. John Dorrance and his brother Arthur had, by concentrating on a single product, managed the metamorphosis of a small, undistinguished cannery into the world's largest manufacturer of canned soup. In the future the company would increase its business by using two strategies: growth and a well-thought-out diversification. Together, these strategies would transform it into one of the world's most successful manufacturers of prepared foods of all kinds.

Right and opposite: With wartime manpower shortages making it difficult to hire the extra workers needed during harvesting season, available members of the Armed Forces volunteered to help Campbell load, sort, and ship tomato products.

An Era of Growth

Arthur Dorrance had never shown any real fondness for Campbell's Tomato Juice. It was not the taste that bothered him; he considered the juice, like all other Campbell products, the highest quality of its kind on the market. Nor did he reject the logic that in 1931 had led Campbell to introduce Tomato Juice. The company's intensive agricultural program had been extremely successful; high-quality tomatoes were abundant, and since the tomato-processing facility was running so efficiently, it made perfect sense to manufacture Tomato Juice along with Tomato Soup.

Dorrance looked unfavorably on the product because he considered it a commodity, not a prepared food, and thus subject to the average consumer's belief that the only thing that distinguished one "brand" from another was

price. In other words, even with the powerfully attractive Campbell's label, shoppers, thinking that all tomato juices were alike, might just reach for the cheapest can. Before his death Dorrance had discussed this issue with his executive vice president, W. B. Murphy, one of whose responsibilities was product development and expansion.

Murphy had already had a hand in Campbell's venture into the mushroom-growing business. For most of its history the company had relied on growers in Kennett Square, Pennsylvania, for the mushrooms needed for its products, especially for the very important Cream of Mushroom Soup. By this time, however, a Campbell plant had been constructed in Sacramento, California, and the cost of shipping mushrooms there and to the

Chicago facility from Pennsylvania was prohibitive. So, a mushroom farm was opened in Prince Crossing, Illinois, to supply the Chicago factory and another was started in Gazos Creek, California, to provide mushrooms for Sacramento.

Murphy's analysis of the tomato juice problem took a different turn. Shortly after the war ended, Campbell began negotiating with Standard Brands to purchase its V8 vegetable juice business. (V8 was originally spelled with a hyphen, but some years after Campbell took it over the hyphen was deleted.) V8, as its name suggests, is a blend of the juices of eight vegetables along with several flavor-enhancing spices. As such, it is a prepared food, not a commodity. It was also a product that would, in Murphy's estimation, fit perfectly into Campbell's

V-8 Vegetable Juices: a magic blend of the juices of the Campbell Tomato, celery, watercress, beets, spinach, lettuce, carrots, and parsley.

8-juice tempter

Even <u>livelier</u> <u>flavor</u> than tomato juice!

Even <u>fewer</u> <u>calories</u> than fruit juice!

If you're of the "old school" of juice drinkers . . . the single juice folks . . . you have a happy day in store.

That's the day you meet V-8! It's 8 fresh vegetable juices squeezed into one. So it's 8 ways more tempting in flavor—8 ways happier in health than any single juice. And it's worlds apart from any other mixed vegetable juice . . . because only Campbell's makes V-8!

So, for goodness' sake . . . both in flavor and health . . . why don't you switch to V-8. A big, chilly glass tastes tempting . . . *any* time of day.

Nature it's wholesome . . . by *Campbell's* **it's delicious!**

V-8
Cocktail
VEGETABLE JUICES

V-8 is a trademark owned by the makers of Campbell's Soups

JTED IN U.S.A.

8-56

Below: Campbell began manufacturing Tomato Juice in 1931.

line, both in terms of marketing (its sales could be reinforced by Campbell's reputation for quality) and manufacture (with a little retooling the tomato-processing plant could produce V8 vegetable juice).

V8 had been invented in 1933 by W. G. Peacock and his son. Both were aware that the public was always attracted by products associated with good health, so they decided to can and bottle vegetable juices such as carrot, spinach, lettuce, celery, and watercress. In the words of one food historian, "In marketing these products, it was found that most of them were so unpalatable that their acceptance was limited to the first purchase." But the Peacocks did not give up. They decided to combine vegetable juices, and after about a year they came up with a product they called Veg-min. At one of the first grocery stores they visited, a clerk, seeing the V for vegetable and the 8 for the eight vegetable juices on the label, suggested they

rename it V8. In 1938, in need of cash to pursue other ideas, the Peacocks sold the formula and trade name to the Louden Packing Company, which upgraded V8 and marketed it until 1943, when Louden was purchased by Standard Brands.

The Campbell management team was extremely interested in this product (it was not a commodity, after all), and after three years of negotiations with Standard Brands, the company finally acquired V8 in 1948. At the time of the purchase the volume of V8 sales was less than five million dollars a year; to raise that figure, Campbell began making adjustments. Improvements were made in the quality and uniformity of the juice. (Campbell had been admired for making every can of soup consistent and thus had a very low return ratio.) Progress was also made in labeling and packaging.

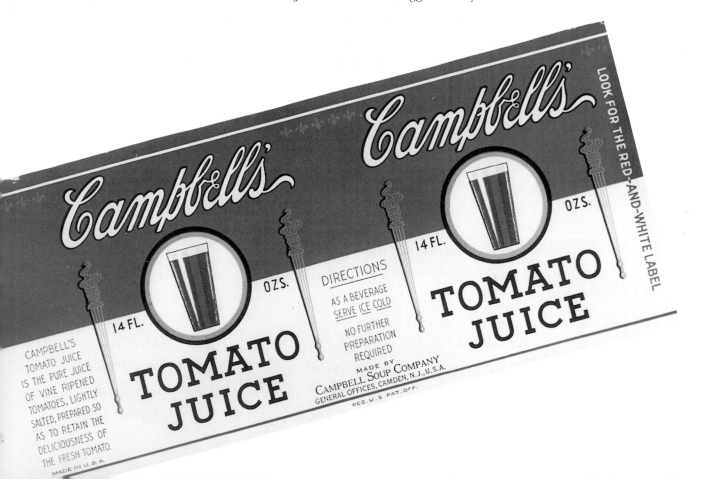

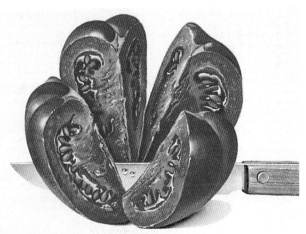

The Campbell Tomato
when it's red outside, it's red clean through

Above: As it had since the days when John Dorrance grew them in his front yard, Campbell agriculturists continued to look for ways to improve upon the color, taste, and texture of tomatoes.

With the exception of the very early days, when the tinsmith Abraham Anderson ran the company, for most of its early history Campbell had purchased its cans, most notably from the Continental Can Company, for which it built plants next to the Chicago and Camden factories in the late twenties. In 1936, thinking it could do the job just as well, the company took over these two plants, and by the late forties Campbell Soup was the third largest manufacturer of cans in the world.

Once Campbell had raised the manufacture of V8 juice to its high standards, it began energetically to advertise this "true specialty in the food field," using, among others, the movie actor Ronald Reagan as one of its spokesmen. Within a few years after Campbell bought V8, sales began to rise dramatically, and it has since remained one of the company's most popular products.

V8 brand was Campbell's first acquisition since the purchase of Franco-American almost thirty-five years earlier. Historically, however, the Franco-American brand and the products associated with it played an odd and relatively small part in the company's business strategy. Once acquired, its ready-to-serve soup line was allowed to languish, and by the early 1940s all that was left of this once well-known brand was Franco-American canned Spaghetti à la Milanaise, which even in those non-pasta-eating times was a fairly popular

Photographed in Paris.   Checking the fine points of a recipe after lunch.

Flavor Scouts

How Campbell travels the world to examine and compare flavors for you

If you really pride yourself on your cooking, you'd probably give your eyeteeth to be able to swap notes with the leading creative chefs of Europe and this country.

Think of the cooking secrets, new combinations of ingredients, flavor tricks, and new or unusual ingredients they could tell you about.

Well, swapping notes with outstanding chefs and sampling their cooking is the pleasant job of the men that we call Campbell Flavor Scouts. They have a wide knowledge of cookery. Just by looking, sniffing and tasting, they can usually identify even the most subtle ingredients in a soup or sauce.

Whenever any chef creates a flavor that wins a reputation, he shouldn't be too surprised to get a visit from a Campbell Flavor Scout. These men don't confine themselves to the big restaurants. They sample the locally famous specialties of little out-of-the-way places like the small French restaurant in the picture, too. In addition, they comb countless cookbooks.

The reason for their work is this: To be certain that the flavor of every good food from the Campbell Kitchens is as fine as the cooking lore of the world knows how to make it. (This is a difficult goal but it's not impossible when Campbell blending skill gets to work with the best ingredients.) In this way, our Flavor Scouts make sure that we practice what we preach when we say: *"To make the best, begin with the best—then cook with extra care."*

"We blend the best with careful pains / In skillful explanation, / And every single can contains / Our famous reputation."

Campbell's

Soups • Tomato Juice • Pork & Beans
V-8 Cocktail Vegetable Juices
Franco-American Products
Swanson Products, including "TV" Brand Dinners

Above: Advertisement for Campbell's Soups and Franco-American Spaghetti, 1956.

dish but not one that matched soup or beans in sales.

The reinvigoration of Franco-American began in 1947 with the reintroduction of Macaroni and Cheese, which had initially been marketed before World War II, and the creation of a new product, Beef Gravy, which was targeted at the postwar housewife who, busy with other obligations, could simply heat up a can to accompany the family dinner. With the success of this first canned gravy, others such as Mushroom Beef were offered, and the once-prominent Franco-American line, the oldest of Campbell's brands, was given new life.

In 1945 the firm had also tentatively entered the baby food market with Campbell's Baby Soups. Though they were reasonably successful, the company soon realized that to compete satisfactorily with the other major manufacturers of baby food it would have to offer a complete line of children's meals. It negotiated for a time with Clapp, a baby food company, which was interested in a merger, but those talks fell through. At the same time the company was also having trouble with the supply of glass baby food jars, so in 1948 Campbell simply decided to get out of the baby food business altogether.

All of these ventures were financed, not by borrowing, but by profits earned from sales, mostly of soup, which accounted for 75 percent of Campbell's business. In fact, Campbell was entirely free of debt, not having borrowed at all since 1904. By the early 1950s Campbell's sales figures were topped by only two other giants in the food-processing industry, General Foods and Standard Brands, both of which had much more extensive product lines. Indeed, in terms of profit margins, Campbell actually outperformed these two companies (while General Foods earned 8 percent on sales before taxes and Standard Brands 5 percent, Campbell earned 15 percent, or fifty-two million dollars, in 1954).

In most ways the company was run exactly as it had been under John and Arthur Dorrance, that is to say tightly, quietly, and conservatively. The offices were located in a large, high-ceilinged, open room on the sixth floor of the Camden factory. Other than that of the president, who occupied the large space originally constructed by Dr. John Dorrance, there were no private offices. Even executives at the vice-presidential level sat at ordinary oak desks, separated from each other by bookcases and filing cabinets. Campbell's management hardly ever left these desks. (Until 1944 all employees, with the single exception of the president, were required to punch a time clock.) They were not encouraged to go to industry conventions nor, except when absolutely necessary, to join associations or societies. The senior executives did not even leave the premises for lunch. They dined each day with the president in a private dining room just off one of the factory's cafeterias.

This corporate style perfectly matched the longtime principles of operation followed by the Campbell Soup Company. These principles, as put in written form by Dr. Dorrance in the early 1920s, were simple, spare, and utilitarian:

1st — To produce products of uniformly superlative quality.

2nd — To develop for itself, by means of advertising, the quality of getting and holding an immense group of buyers to whom its label is a guarantee of satisfaction.

3rd — The building of prestige, first through the satisfaction of the customers, second, through the character of the Company as an institution, and third, through the character of the individuals who compose its organization.

Though this code of business conduct remained fixed, major changes in management, ownership, and size lay ahead. Since the death of Arthur Dorrance, James McGowan had served as president. In 1953, when McGowan

retired, Murphy was appointed president, only the fourth in the history of
the Campbell Soup Company.

The following year an even bigger
change occurred, this time in ownership. Since the death of Dr. Dorrance
in 1930, the Campbell Soup Company
had been privately owned by the
Dorrance Estate. In the early 1950s,
however, it was decided that stock in
the company would for the first time
be publicly offered. The estate did
this for several reasons: to diversify its
holdings, to establish a market value
for Campbell's stock, and to make
shares available to salaried workers.
Besides, shareholders could help if the
company ever needed to argue its case
before the government, as it had
during World War II when tin-plate
allocations were being handed out.
Thus, in November 1954, Campbell

stock was traded for the first time,
making it a publicly held corporation,
at least in name (the estate still owned
85 percent of the company).

Through the 1950s Campbell, like
the entire country, enjoyed growth and
prosperity. Consumers had money to
spend and the demand for new products, particularly those that promised
convenience, was huge. After breaking
the "twenty-one kinds" barrier in the
late 1930s, Campbell began adding
new soups to its line almost yearly.
Several of these lasted only a few years
— Cream of Spinach and Cream of
Vegetable, for instance — but many
continue to be manufactured to this
day: Onion, Chicken Vegetable,
Turkey Noodle, Minestrone, Tomato
with Rice.

It was also during this era that
Campbell began relying more and

more on its home economics department. When the company first began to make soup, there was no home economist on the staff. Dr. John Dorrance, the trained chef and gourmet, made all decisions concerning soup varieties and their use in meals. In turn, Arthur Dorrance, whose culinary sophistication matched that of his brother, also made all determinations about kinds and quality. In the late thirties, however, the first sales-research department was formed, and one of its units, home economics, was charged with discovering "what housewives like in food products" and "encouraging the use of Campbell's products."

The home economists also were responsible for writing Campbell cookbooks. In 1941, with the publication of *Easy Ways to Good Meals* by Ann

Marshall, later replaced by Carolyn Campbell, the noms de plume of the collective home economics department, Campbell began a run of increasingly longer and more complete cookbooks. By the 1950s about a million of these were in print at any one time, with titles such as *Cooking with Condensed Soup, Wonderful Ways with Soups,* and *Campbell's Treasury of Recipes.*

The fifties were the heyday of the meat-and-potatoes era in American cookery, a fact reflected in the names of the dishes included in the 1952 version of *Cooking with Condensed Soup*: Mushroom Meatballs, Party-going Pork Chops, Heavenly Ham Loaf, Especially Good Creamed Chicken, and Festive Franks. Despite the silliness of these names, the recipes reflect a fairly significant shift away from gravy as the principal flavoring liquid and toward

Above: During the early 1950s Campbell periodically introduced new varieties of soup: one of the most popular was Onion. Opposite: Campbell executives in the 1950s, including even President William B. Murphy, made regular visits to the test kitchens to sample new varieties and to make sure that standard soups remained as they should taste. Photographer Dan Weiner captured the moment.

what was, for many families, a novel and revolutionary use of what would traditionally be called a sauce. This shift was so radical that, as the food writer Jo Brans reports, children of many traditional families — those who ate the same meal, "meat, potatoes, salad and milk, six nights out of seven" — often feared that when visiting friends they would be forced to eat "funny food, like lasagna or tuna fish casserole, or some strange vegetable."

The recipes for many of these "funny foods" came straight from Campbell's cookbooks. Most young American women, who had been taught to cook by their mothers, had no idea how to make a sauce. (The typical housewife of the time usually owned only one cookbook, which she rarely used.) The wide circulation of Campbell cookbooks changed that. With one of these simple recipes in hand, the housewife could, by opening a can of Campbell's Soup, make a "Perfect Tuna Casserole," the classic recipe for which, as printed in *Wonderful Ways with Soups* is as follows:

*1 can (10 1/2 ounces) condensed
   Cream of Celery or
   Mushroom Soup*
1/2 cup milk
*1 can (7 ounces) tuna, drained
   and flaked*
1 cup cooked peas or green beans
*1 1/4 cups slightly crumbled
   potato chips*

Blend soup and milk; stir in tuna, peas, and 1 cup potato chips. Spoon into a 1-quart casserole. Sprinkle top with remaining potato chips. If desired, use whole chips on top of casserole rather than crumbled. Bake in a moderate oven (375°F.) about 25 minutes. Makes 3 or 4 servings.

Stripped of its now-famous name, Perfect Tuna Casserole is no more or less than fish cooked in a white sauce, the top of which has been gratinéed, or made crispy. The same is generally true of many of the other famous Campbell dishes of the era: Chicken Divan (sliced chicken, broccoli, Cream of Mushroom Soup and cheddar cheese); Chicken in Mushroom and Wine Sauce (chicken breasts, onions, Cream of Mushroom Soup, and sherry, optional); or even Green Bean Bake

(green beans, Cream of Mushroom Soup, and a can of French-fried onions). In other words, surprising as it may now seem, these "funny foods" were actually fancy foods, dishes like those made famous in France that used sauces rather than traditional American gravies or condiments such as ketchup, mustard, or steak sauce.

Other of the recipes in *Wonderful Ways with Soups* ventured even farther from standard American fare and introduced international dishes such as Swedish Meatballs, Lamb Curry, Veal Parmesan, and Chicken Paprika. In some cases, the book even suggested that the housewife attempt a sauce of her own. For example, recipes were given for Mock Hollandaise, Tomato Horseradish Sauce, Poulette Sauce, and Mushroom Almond Sauce, the recipe for which is:

1/4 cup chopped blanched almonds
2 tablespoons butter or margarine
1 can (10 1/2 ounces) condensed
  Cream of Mushroom Soup
1/3 cup water
1 tablespoon minced onion
1 tablespoon sherry (optional)

In saucepan, lightly brown almonds in butter. Blend in soup, water, onion, and sherry. Simmer, stirring often, for a few minutes. Especially good on fish, asparagus, and chicken. Makes about 1 1/2 cups sauce.

Campbell's recipes for soup as a stand-alone dish were also fairly unusual for the times. Bean with Bacon Treat, for instance, was a mixture of sausage links, Bean with Bacon Soup, and cubes of red apple. Another such

recipe, perhaps harder to imagine, was for Peanut Butter Bisque, which called for onion, butter, peanut butter, Cream of Chicken Soup, and minced parsley, celery, or grated carrot. *Wonderful Ways with Soups* also introduced the idea of Soup Mates, a mixture of "two soups to make a new soup that's personally your own."

The mixing of canned soups was, at least among gourmets, a fairly common notion. It was recommended by M. F. K. Fisher in her classic 1942

♦♦♦

On these and the following pages are photographs from a second major article on Campbell Soup Company published by *Fortune* magazine twenty years after the first. In 1955 the first-rate photojournalist Dan Weiner covered the manufacturing processes and discovered, as Bourke-White had, that hand labor was still essential to the preparation and inspection of ingredients for Campbell's soups.

volume *How to Cook a Wolf*, and according to Louis P. De Gouy, who had apprenticed under Escoffier, "teaming a couple of cans of soup" was a common practice among restaurant chefs. In his 1949 book on soup he wrote,

This is often done in first-class restaurants. Because of the canned soups available in every town in the land, it is very easy for even a busy cook to fix a bowl of delicious soup in a hurry. Some cooks think so highly of many canned soups that they do very little to fancy them up. However, there are some little tricks that make a soup taste as if the cook had spent all afternoon over it. A bit of sherry or claret can be added to a can of meat stock and to some vegetable soups. A dab of sour cream floating in the center of a plate of tomato soup is an addition that has been found successful. A sprinkling of grated cheese (any kind), or some mixed herbs, makes a good canned soup taste like an inspired concoction, be it called soup or potage.

The best known of these Soup Mates was probably Purée Mongole, a mixture of Pea and Tomato, but others included Rosy Beef Noodle Twosome (Beef Noodle and Tomato), Gardener's Clam Chowder (Clam Chowder and Green Pea), and Creamy Gumbo (Cream of Chicken and Chicken Gumbo). There were even several recipes for "hearties," which combined three soups; Green Velvet, for instance, mixed Cream of Mushroom, Cream of Asparagus, and Cream of Chicken.

Wonderful Ways with Soups also included recipes for "foreign fare," made with Campbell's Soup. These included Greek Soup, Mexicali Soup, Borsch, and Polish Soup, which called for:

1 cup diced potatoes
1/4 cup thinly sliced onion
2 tablespoons butter or margarine
1 tablespoon chopped parsley
1 tablespoon chopped pimento
1/2 teaspoon paprika
1 can (10 1/2 ounces) condensed
*   Consommé*
1/2 soup can water
Sour cream

Cook potatoes and onion in butter until onion is lightly browned. Stir in parsley, pimento, and paprika. Add Consommé and water. Cover; simmer until potatoes are done, about 10 minutes. Garnish each serving with sour cream. Makes 2 or 3 servings.

Not all of these suggestions and recipes became standard fare, of course, but some of those that did have now become classics of a sort. Cooks found

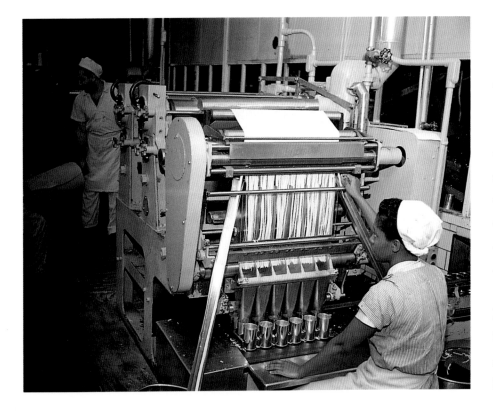

that dishes such as Perfect Tuna
Casserole, Green Bean Bake, and
Souperburgers (skillet ground-beef
dishes that used a Campbell's Soup
as a sauce), were extremely easy to
make and served as an excellent
alternative to the meat-and-potatoes
meals they usually put on the table.
It took a while, but in time even
children grew to like these "funny
foods." In fact, in many American
families one night a week was usually called "tuna casserole night" or
"Souperburger night."

As effective as these cookbooks
were in convincing housewives to use
soup, they were obviously not the
only method of selling the product.
Advertising remained, as it had been
from the first days of the company,
the major marketing vehicle, and
television, then a brand-new medium,
became, along with print ads, the best
way to reach the average consumer.
"Our whole business," the company
said at the time, "is making public
goodwill: that is, the degree of pleasure
that consumers get out of our prod-

Above: Dan Weiner found that a kettle of ingredients was still blended by hand in 1955. Left: A chef works with much smaller quantities in the test kitchen.

ucts." This philosophy, of course, was as old as the company itself, which had, since the turn of the century, directed the preponderance of its attention, not at wholesalers or retailers, but straight at the consumer. "Our publication and broadcast advertising," Campbell explained, "is a nucleus for the creation of public goodwill."

There were, however, some major changes made in the manner and method of Campbell's advertising strategy. For the previous forty years the company had had only one advertising agency, Ward Wheelock, located in Philadelphia. Likewise, Wheelock had had only one account, Campbell Soup. But Wheelock was a relatively small agency, and Campbell executives thought that its lack of manpower made it no longer adequate to the growing company's needs. They told this to Wheelock, adding that they would give him as long as a year and a half to find a way to provide more service. For whatever reason, Wheelock decided not to expand, and in 1954 Campbell transferred its accounts to a number of other advertising agencies: soup to BBDO; Franco-American to Ogilvy, Benson and Mather; Pork and Beans and V8 to Needham, Louis & Brorby; and overall quality and children's advertising to Leo Burnett.

This last campaign, to speak directly to children, was the predicate for other changes in advertising tactics. The first of these involved the revitalization and modernization of the Campbell Kids. The gradual downplaying of the Kids reached its nadir in 1951, when the Kids appeared in fewer than 10 percent of the company's advertisements. That year, however,

with the new children's campaign in mind, it was decided to make extensive use of them once again in ads and licensed products.

First the Kids needed to be slightly updated. Over the years they had been drawn by a number of people both in and out of the company: Corinne Pauli, members of Ward Wheelock's staff, and the Paul Fennel Agency. In 1951 the Johnston and Cushing Studios in New York and the Hurrell-Disney Studios in California were chosen to create new Kids. Everyone was apprehensive. As Leo Burnett said, "The Kids can be doing modern things and wear modern clothes, but any attempt to change their chubby, cherubic, rosy-cheeked faces would be like having a Scottie

Below: Two of the many Campbell recipe books that provided guidance for using soups to create numerous other dishes.

or a cairn instead of a fox terrier listening to His Master's Voice."

Changes, however slight to most viewers, were made, and the next task was the reintroduction of the updated Kids in both ads and promotions. The Campbell Kids had been manufactured as dolls since 1910, when E. I. Horsman had offered the first official ones for a dollar apiece. Throughout the teens and on into the forties, Campbell Kids dolls were marketed by a variety of companies (Horsman, Montgomery Ward, Sears) in a number of sizes (eleven to sixteen inches in height), styles (peekaboo, petite, little Dutch girl), and compositions (bisque, cloth, and "Can't Break 'Em" material). Most are now collector's items and sell for high prices in the antique doll market.

In 1954, the fiftieth birthday of the Kids, Campbell licensed thirty-four manufacturers to produce Campbell Kids products, a promotion that was inaugurated by a seven-page spread in *Life* magazine. The firm did not ask for royalties on any of these, believing that their sale and circulation represented fairly inexpensive advertising, and within a couple of years Campbell products included rubber stamps, toy electric mixers and vacuum cleaners, wallpaper, wading pools, yo-yos, beach balls, and Campbell Kids cooking sets, complete with miniature cans of Campbell's Tomato and Beef Soups, Pork & Beans, and Franco-American Spaghetti. All of this effort climaxed when 560,000 Campbell Kids dolls, the first offered by the company itself, were sold as a premium for a dollar each.

The Kids also showed up in Campbell's newest advertising medium, television. Throughout the forties the company had fairly consistently divided its advertising dollar, spending twice as much on radio as it did on print advertisements. This changed when television came along. In 1954, for instance, about $6 million was budgeted for magazines and Sunday supplements, $4.5 million for television, and just about $1 million for radio. At first Campbell sponsored general-interest television shows such as "Henry Morgan's Great Talent Hunt," "The Aldrich Family," and "The Campbell Sound Stage." However, in tune with its emphasis on the children's market, the company soon shifted to programs such as "The Howdy Doody Show," "The Mickey Mouse Club," and "Lassie." (One longtime Campbell sales executive was

The *Campbell Soup Kids* are going places !

The kids that folks have held so dear
  For well nigh onto fifty year
Are now adorning things galore
  For homes, for boys, for girls...and more.
Come celebrate their birthday.... <u>and</u>
  Have fun in stores throughout the land !

C'mon along to the next page! to see a few of the many, many Campbell Kids products. You'll know they're the finest of their kind!

at first slightly suspicious of the latter's appeal. "Take away the kid and the dog," he is reported to have said, "and what have you got?") Campbell's advertisements, whether in print or on radio or television, typically included a jingle. The little four-line poems that had accompanied prewar ads were gone, and in their place were ditties such as "Soup This Good Just Has to Be Campbell's," "Sing a Song of Soup Sense," and "Have You, Have You Had Your Soup Today?/ Campbell's of Course/Campbell's of Course." Most of these jingles were devised by copywriters working for one or another of the advertising agencies hired by Campbell, but the name of the author of the most famous one of all is lost.

Sometime during the thirties, it is guessed, somebody spontaneously came up with the phrase "M'm! M'm! Good!," to describe Campbell's Soup. Shortly thereafter, an entire lyric was created: "M'm! M'm! Good!/ M'm! M'm! Good! / That's What Campbell's Soups Are/M'm! M'm! Good!" The rhythmic and mnemonic qualities of this little song were so compelling that, despite dozens of other campaign slogans, it has lasted for more than fifty years. (To understand why, compare it with one of the clunkier and less memorable jingles of the postwar era: "They Always Eat Better When You Remember the Soup.")

Not all of Campbell's sales efforts during the 1950s were so successful. Three of its less successful ventures are, however, interesting for what they say about the company and the buying and eating habits of the American public.

Above: In 1950 Campbell first entered the field of television advertising and in 1954 it sponsored "Lassie." Another popular fifties television program was "The Donna Reed Show," which Campbell began sponsoring in 1958.

The first of these products was FR-8, which, like its vegetable counterpart V8, was a blend of the juices of eight fruits. FR-8 seemed like a terrific idea, but when it was test marketed in homes around the country the response was negative. Why? There was a simple explanation from Campbell's executives: "We never could get the product right." In other words, its taste appeal did not match that of single juices, and after a couple of years FR-8 was withdrawn.

Other new product efforts of the period were fruit soups. For some time a campaign had been underway to introduce the concept of cold soups to the American public. *Wonderful Ways with Soups* had given several recipes, arguing that "for summertime and something special anytime, frosty cold soups and jellied consommé make delightful appetizers or entrees." On the whole, however, the public did not buy the idea, and at the time few served Vichyssoise, Gazpacho, or a cold soup Campbell called Shrimp Pink Ice. Pretty much the same prejudice was held against fruit soups which, despite their refreshing flavors and the fact that they were extremely popular in places like Scandinavia, simply did not sell in America.

The last of these new fifties inspirations was frozen soup. The virtues of freezing had been studied since the mid-nineteenth century, and it was well known that in some cases this technique was better able to retain flavor, appearance, texture, and nutritional value than other methods of food preservation. By the mid-thirties many fruits and vegetables were commercially frozen, but there were several problems with the business. Neither grocery stores nor their customers necessarily had the facilities to store frozen foods. Following World War I there was a flurry of interest in locker plants — huge freezer facilities, sections of which could be rented by private individuals. But the enthusiasm for locker plants died out after World War II when refrigerator manufacturers introduced home freezers.

Frozen soups, Campbell thought, were a perfect accompaniment to the home freezer trend. Most of the ones

marketed were fish soups such as Oyster Stew and Cream of Shrimp, the delicate flavors of which were more easily retained by freezing. The company was very excited about this new line. The soups were test marketed successfully, and money was committed to television and print advertising. Frozen soup, unlike FR-8, was a very good-tasting product, but it too failed to gain general acceptance. Why? No one was quite sure. Perhaps Campbell's own good products contributed to the problem. The best explanation is that a country that had grown up on Campbell's canned soups was not ready to give up that habit, even though the new soups were tasty and carried the familiar label. A few years after their introduction, Campbell's frozen soups for home consumption were discontinued.

This setback, however, did not mark the end of the company's involvement in the frozen-food industry. In May 1955, six months after Campbell had gone public, it acquired C. A. Swanson & Sons, a large Omaha, Nebraska, canning and freezing firm. Swanson was an old company, almost as old as Campbell, begun in 1899 by a twenty-year-old immigrant who had arrived in this country with a tag around his neck that read "Carl Swanson, Swedish. Send me to Omaha. I speak no English." Young Swanson must have learned the language fairly expeditiously, for three years after his arrival he joined with two other men to form a wholesale food company that handled eggs, milk, butter, and poultry.

Like John Dorrance, Swanson was a hard-working, smart businessman, and

NEW! FR-8 *Blended* FRUIT JUICES

CONTENTS 12 FL. OZ.
MADE IN U.S.A. BY CAMPBELL SOUP COMPANY
GENERAL OFFICES, CAMDEN, N. J.

BLENDED FROM GRAPEFRUIT · ORANGES · PEACHES
APRICOTS · BANANAS · APPLES · LEMONS AND LIMES
With added sugar and natural flavoring

Above: For a time in the early 1950s Campbell test marketed a blended fruit juice called FR-8.

his company prospered first on the local and then on the national level. By 1949 it was grossing over $50 million a year, and he was known as "the biggest butter-and-eggs man in the country." After his death Swanson's two sons, Gilbert and Clarke, continued to enlarge the company's business, taking particular advantage of its expertise in frozen foods, which it had gained while supplying U.S. armed forces with frozen chickens during World War II.

After the war Swanson, primarily a dealer in commodities, began offering its frozen products to retailers, many of whom were beginning to install freezer compartments in their grocery stores. The first were uncooked frozen chickens, but in 1951 it introduced its first prepared foods, frozen chicken, beef, and turkey pot pies. Then the Swanson brothers had an even better idea: why not freeze and sell an entire dinner? They turned to Betty Cronin, a young bacteriologist on their staff, who by 1954 was able to create two dinners: turkey and pot roast, each complete with the trimmings.

Creating such a dinner was not as easy as it sounds, of course. Packed together in a compartmentalized aluminum tray, all items had to come out of the oven hot, evenly cooked, and ready to eat. Additionally, with the fried chicken dinner, which it took Cronin until 1955 to perfect, there was the problem of ingredients like the

Below and opposite: During the
late 1950s and early 1960s Campbell
marketed a line of frozen soups.

breading. "What kind of breading," Cronin recalled, "will stay on through freezing, not be too greasy, and still taste good?"

These first prepared meals were called "TV dinners," after another great phenomenon of the age. In fact, television was so popular that it altered the eating habits of many families. As Cronin said: "You had ten people gathered around a little screen, so you couldn't sit at a table. Things seemed to be going toward lap-eating." The upshot of this trend, as food writer Jo Brans has suggested, was that "TV dinners, with every individual dinner heated in the oven and served on TV trays in front of the TV set, were the essence of modernity." (Indeed, the dinners were packed in boxes illustrated to look like televisions, complete with screen, wood cabinet, and volume and channel knobs.)

At the time of the buyout by Campbell, Swanson was still very much in the commodities business, selling dairy products, poultry, ice, and commercial animal feed. These parts of the

company were liquidated. It was, after all, the specialty frozen foods for the consumer that the company was interested in. Much of the product research was shifted to Camden, and over time new Swanson frozen products such as Macaroni and Beef, and Noodles and Chicken were introduced. (Betty Cronin also moved, becoming one of Campbell's chief experts on American cooking and eating habits.) Campbell's philosophy of acquisition, as with Swanson and others, was fairly simple. The management sought to develop products or acquire companies where Campbell had considerable expertise and where there was the opportunity for major expansion. Most companies that fit this definition were probably well run and thus would blend nicely with longtime Campbell principles of operation. "If the company has high-quality products, has sound internal and external operating policies, is conducted in an aggressive way, and is making good products, you can accept the fact that management has been effective."

No company better met these standards than Pepperidge Farm, which manufactured very high-quality bakery products; indeed, they were known as top-of-the-line, relatively high-ticket items. Though it was a medium-size company, distributing in only a few sections of the country, Pepperidge Farm was quite profitable, and under the leadership of its founder and president, Margaret Rudkin, it was clearly well run.

Like Campbell, Pepperidge Farm grew from the vision and experience of its founder. Rudkin, who was married to a successful Wall Street broker, had

he famous New Orleans restaurants never made it better!

Campbell's frozen
CREAM of SHRIMP

A great seacoast delicacy, now yours any time or place— thanks to freezing!

Even in New Orleans, you'd look a long time before you found Cream of Shrimp soup to compare with the kind that Campbell's can now set before you, through freezing.

Campbell's makes it with choice shrimp, plenty of cream, butter, and a pinch or two of special seasonings and spices. All brought together in a perfect blend and balance—thanks to freezing!

Freezing . . . that's how Campbell's can now bring you this real party-going soup in prepared form, just any time you take the notion. It's right there in your grocer's freezer—Campbell's Frozen Cream of Shrimp Soup.

Campbell's frozen soups

Oyster Stew • Green Pea with Ham • Cream of Potato • Cream of Shrimp

Above: In 1955 Campbell purchased C. A. Swanson & Sons and shortly afterward introduced a number of improved heat-and-serve TV dinners. An example of the Swanson aluminum TV dinner tray is now in the collection of the Smithsonian Institution.

always been interested in nutrition, especially that of young children. In 1937 when her nine-year-old son was diagnosed as having severe asthma, this interest deepened. As she told the story:

The doctors ordered that we have one of two things: a diet strong in natural vitamin B, or a change in climate. Moving across the country with my three sons, husband, assorted dogs, cats and horses was impossible. And, as I soon discovered, so was finding products and particularly bread with the right vitamin B content. I wanted bread

made with old-fashioned stone-ground, whole-wheat flour. I visited store after store. Everywhere the story was the same. "Sorry, madam, we haven't carried anything like that for a generation. Nobody bakes such bread anymore."

Actually, the prejudice against whole-wheat flour stretched back considerably more than just a generation. The fifth-century-B.C. writer Archestratus, expressing his preference for white over dark bread, wrote that "among the others [breads] the best can be found on Lesbos, and there on the sailors' hill bathed by the billows, where the illustrious Eresus is: bread so white it outdoes the ethereal snow in purity." White bread continued to be preferred through the Middle Ages, when, because of the extra expense of milling the bran out of the flour, it became a luxury item and its appearance on the dining table a status symbol. This partiality became even more apparent in the twentieth century when huge, fast, and efficient machines that ground grain with steel blades almost entirely replaced the stone wheels of the old-fashioned grist mill. Now white bread could be manufactured cheaply. Despite a mid-nineteenth-century campaign conducted by the Reverend Sylvester Graham, who argued that removing the bran from flour was "putting asunder what God has joined together," whole-wheat bread never had a chance when put up against cheap, factory-baked loaves of white.

Plainly, Rudkin was not discouraged by the fact that nutritious whole-wheat bread was nearly impossible to purchase. She decided to bake some herself. Unable at first to find a grist mill to supply her with flour, she ground the wheat herself in a coffee grinder. Then, using a recipe handed down to her from her grandmother, she baked her first loaf of bread. She would recall that it "should have been sent to the Smithsonian Institution as a sample of bread from the Stone Age, for it was hard as a rock and about one inch high."

After several more tries Rudkin came up with a loaf of whole-wheat bread which, made with butter, milk, honey, and molasses, was not only good for her son but also tasted good. As she remembered:

Now Dad's an expert at "fryin' up" a chicken dinner!

Dad's night to cook is only one of so many special occasions when a delicious Swanson TV Brand Dinner answers your problems. It's just as handy when the teen-agers take over on a weekend, or when Mom's tired from shopping with the youngsters. It's all cooked, frozen, and ready to heat in its own individual serving tray—without thawing. So there's no work before—no dishes after. But how good it tastes—Swanson's extra-meaty, extra-tender golden-fried chicken with garden-fresh mixed vegetables and fluffy mashed potatoes. Don't wait—have some tonight.

Only Swanson has the secret of these delicious well-balanced TV Brand Dinners.

Also try Swanson TV Brand Turkey and Beef Dinners

Swanson
TV BRAND DINNERS
MADE ONLY BY C. A. SWANSON & SONS. A SUBSIDIARY OF CAMPBELL SOUP COMPANY

All the family liked it, and pretty soon we ate nothing but homemade whole-wheat bread. When I told the doctor I was making bread from stone-ground flour, he wouldn't believe me because he said it was too coarse and I would have to add white flour to it. To convince him, I brought him some samples and told him exactly what I put in with the flour. Immediately he wanted to order it for himself and for his other patients.

Above: Swanson TV Dinner advertisement, 1960.

157

The doctor was not the only one who loved Rudkin's bread. Friends and neighbors were constantly asking to buy loaves. Why not also sell it through grocery stores? they suggested. Though Rudkin had no business experience, she totaled up the cost of making her bread and approached local merchants, who informed her that no one would pay the twenty-five cents she would have to charge. "They will if the loaf is worth twenty-five cents," Rudkin answered, and she was correct. The first local store to carry her bread sold out its entire stock within hours, and the first New York grocer she approached very quickly increased his order from a few to two hundred loaves a day. (In the early days her husband delivered the bread to New York City by setting a box next to him on the train.)

Within months Rudkin found herself in the commercial bakery business. At first, to keep up the supply, she cleared a space in her garage, retrieved a stove and some nursery scales from the basement, and hired a local girl to help. When production needs called for even more space, the bakery was moved to an unused stable. By September 1938, the end of her first year in business, Rudkin's home bakery was producing four thousand loaves a week. She was no longer a housewife baking a few loaves of bread in her spare time; she was a businesswoman, the owner and operator of a growing company that she named Pepperidge Farm, after the pepperidge trees that grew in the yard of her Connecticut home.

Rudkin borrowed fifteen thousand dollars, rented two Norwalk, Connecti-

Opposite: After baking loaves of wholesome whole-wheat bread for her family in 1937, Margaret Rudkin found that the demand for her bread was so strong that within three years she began selling her product to local grocery stores. Above and below: Pepperidge Farm was the name of her family's home in Connecticut.

cut, buildings, lined up distributors, and within several years was running a business that employed over a hundred people and baked ten thousand loaves a day. Other products were added to the Pepperidge Farm line: poultry stuffing, cookies, brown-and-serve rolls, and frozen pastries. As the company grew, new factories were built in Downingtown, Pennsylvania, on the Main Line west of Philadelphia, and in Downer's Grove, Illinois, to serve customers in the Midwest.

By 1960, when Rudkin was approached by Campbell, Pepperidge Farm was shipping over a million loaves of bread a week and earning $1.25 million profit a year on the sales of all its products. After a year or so of negotiations a stock deal was made (Campbell exchanged 360,000 shares of its stock, at $64 dollars per share, for all of the stock in Rudkin's com-

---

Pepperidge Farm

[Part Three]

STANDARD WHITE BREAD
(Makes 2 loaves)

Preheat oven to 400° F., 20 minutes before loaves are ready to bake.

½ cup milk
3 tablespoons sugar
2 teaspoons salt
3 tablespoons butter or margarine
1½ cups warm water
1 package or cake yeast, dry or compressed
5½ cups unsifted flour (about) or 6¼ cups sifted flour (about)

Scald the milk; stir in the sugar, salt and butter or margarine.
Cool to lukewarm.
Measure the warm water into a large bowl; sprinkle or crumble in the yeast.
Stir until dissolved.
Add the lukewarm milk mixture and 3 cups flour; beat until smooth.
Add enough additional flour to make a soft dough.
Turn out onto a lightly floured board.
Knead until smooth and elastic, about 8 to 10 minutes.
Form into a smooth ball.
Place in a greased bowl, turning to grease all sides.
Cover; let rise in a warm place, free from draft, until doubled in bulk, about 1 hour.
Punch down.
Let rest for 15 minutes.
Divide the dough in half.
Shape each half into a loaf.
Place each loaf in a greased bread pan, 9 by 5 by 3 inches.
Place each loaf in a warm place, free from draft, until doubled
let rise in a warm place, free from draft, until doubled
hour. . F.) for about 50 minutes.

pany), and Pepperidge Farm, with Rudkin remaining as its president, became a wholly owned subsidiary of the Campbell Soup Company.

Throughout the 1960s Campbell made further acquisitions, both in America and overseas. In 1960, in order to get a foothold in Australia, it bought the small canned-good maker called the Kia Ora Company, which it used as a base of operations for Kia Ora and Campbell products. The following year it purchased the Delacre Company of Belgium, a longtime manufacturer of biscuits and cookies. (At the time Pepperidge Farm was

paying fairly high royalties on Delacre recipes, and it was recognized that buying the company outright would be less expensive in the long run than continuing to pay these fees.) And in 1969, after becoming interested in the specialty candy business, Campbell purchased the North American rights to produce the chocolates of the famous Godiva Company of Belgium. (Several years later the Godiva owner, Josef Draps, asked Campbell to buy out the entire business, which it eventually did.)

By 1969 the Campbell Soup Company, in one incarnation or other,

Above: In 1961 Campbell acquired
Delacre, a European biscuit company founded in 1869.

had been in business for one hundred years. During this period it had gone through many cycles of expansion and contraction. It had begun as a canner of over two hundred products, first under Joseph Campbell, then Arthur Dorrance, only to be transformed, under Dr. John T. Dorrance, into a manufacturer of only one — condensed soup. Despite the fact that sales grew astronomically, Campbell remained basically a soup company throughout most of its early history; Pork & Beans, Tomato Juice, and Franco-American Spaghetti were only side ventures.

During the post–World War II era, however, the company expanded once again, this time in both sales and the number of products manufactured. In 1958 it grossed $500 million in sales, ten times what it had made thirty years earlier, and by 1969 it was selling, in addition to its expanded soup line, Franco-American Spaghetti, Macaroni, sauces, and gravies; Swanson frozen foods; Pepperidge Farm baked goods; and Godiva chocolates; as well as a line of stews, sauces, and puddings packed under the Bounty label. It had been Dr. Dorrance's ambition to make Campbell the greatest soup company in the world. Now it was that and more: it was one of the largest and most prosperous prepared-food companies in the world.

Above: In 1950 Campbell marketed tomato ketchup with a Kid on the label, one of the few times one was used to advertise a product other than soup. The label dates from 1958. Below: In 1969 Campbell acquired the North American rights to manufacture the chocolates of the Belgian firm Godiva Chocolatier. In 1974 Campbell purchased the entire company and began world-wide production.

Dessert.

Dessert, in its truest sense, is no longer considered an indulgence that can only follow a meal. Not when you can indulge in the spell of Godiva® Chocolate at the merest quirk of temptation. You need only dream of the intriguing shapes and delectable fillings. Then dessert will be at your beck and call. Godiva Chocolates are available in three, two, one and one-half pound assortments, packaged in scintillating golden ballotins.

GODIVA®
Chocolatier
BRUXELLES · NEW YORK
PARIS · COLOGNE

Godiva Chocolatier, 701 Fifth Avenue, New York, New York 10022.

125 Years of Success

One senior Campbell executive referred to him as "that American artist whose life-style was rather unusual." But the artist, Andy Warhol, was, in W. B. Murphy's words "making paintings, color replicas, of a Campbell's Tomato Soup can, and selling them for large sums — up to two thousand dollars." Murphy wondered if "this might do some harm to the company's reputation."

Why Warhol turned to Campbell's Soup as a subject in 1962 is a matter of endless and often bootless debate among art historians. It is conceivable that his motive was, as one critic has speculated, purely art historical, that these "red-and-white-labeled pictures signaled a cold-blooded rebellion against the centuries-long tradition of painterly still lifes." Or maybe Warhol's aim was to produce a piece of socio-

cultural criticism, one that pointed out the utter banality of America by presenting a "humdrum can of condensed soup starkly isolated against a refrigerator-white background."

Perhaps it is best just to take Warhol's word for it. When asked what he thought of Tomato Soup, he answered, "I love it," adding that his mother had served it to him daily, and that the Campbell's Soup habit had endured into adulthood. "I just paint things I always thought were beautiful," Warhol continued, "things you use every day and never think about. I'm working on soups. . . . I just do it because I like it."

In some limited sense, however, Murphy's concern was well founded; Warhol and the Campbell's Soup can had become forever allied, at least in the minds of art historians. "Tomato

soup will never just be tomato soup again," declared the critic Ivan Karp, a comment that, however intellectually adventurous, turned out to be, at least in terms of general consumer appreciation, ridiculous. To the millions who ate Campbell's Tomato Soup, Warhol among them, the reach to take the can off the shelf and the satisfaction of the first spoonful were utterly unaffected by the controversy surrounding the paintings. Furthermore, despite executives' concern, Warhol's work had no discernible effect upon the prosperity or reputation of the Campbell Soup Company. Earnings continued to rise, as they had throughout most of the company's history; there was no falloff in the sales of Tomato or any of the other soups. (Indeed, twenty years later the company commissioned Warhol to make

a print, the subject of which was Campbell's new dry-soup mix.)

The fact was that Campbell's soups had by the 1960s become the gold standard of prepared soups, to which all others were compared. This should not be surprising, especially when the Campbell history is taken into consideration. When Dr. John Dorrance began manufacturing his product in 1897, one of his main problems was that soups of any kind were not a part of the everyday diet. "Few Americans ate soups," one commentator of the time wrote. "For the majority, the very name of soup suggested remnants boiled down to a greasy liquid neither pleasing to the eye nor palatable."

Dr. Dorrance almost single-handedly refashioned this unappetizing, lackluster image. Campbell's Soups were prepared with the best ingredients from the best recipes and by the best culinary operations. They were, in other words, far from banal; they were fresh, novel, and savory; they were the highest quality canned soups money could buy.

More surprisingly, despite the fact that many housewives continued to make one or more specialty soups at home, as time went by few compared these with Campbell's soups. The two varieties were, in the minds of the public, mutually exclusive: homemade soup had its own distinctive taste; Campbell's soups had theirs. If truth be told, Campbell did not compete with homemade for the simple reason that most Campbell's soups were well beyond the expertise of the average cook. Most home cooks did not have the time, and neither the ingredients nor the skill to prepare a soup even as seemingly simple as vegetable and have it taste as good as Campbell's.

The flavors of Campbell's soups had by this time planted themselves deeply in the collective culinary unconscious of the majority of Americans. As Warhol implied, the memories of Campbell's soups, born in childhood, somehow abide, along with those of other favorite family foods, well into adulthood. For every artist like Marcel Proust — whose "remembrances of things past" were triggered by a French pastry — millions had memories called up by the aroma of Vegetable, Tomato, or Chicken Noodle soup heating on the kitchen stove.

Warhol's widely exhibited work and huge international reputation did have one immediate effect on the Campbell Soup Company: it decided

Opposite, above, and below: Soup tureens in pottery, porcelain, and silver highlight the collection of The Campbell Museum. Its inception in 1966 was the brainchild of John T. Dorrance, Jr., and W. B. Murphy, who saw the collection as a vivid way to present the image and lineage of soup. The Campbell Museum has both exhibited and toured its singular collection since 1970.

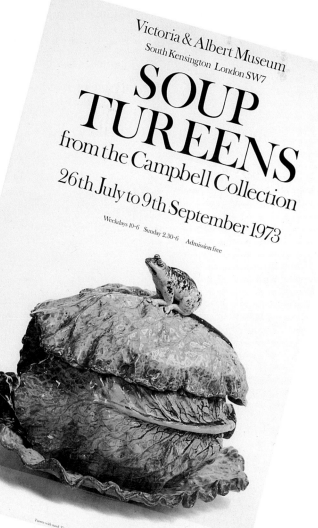

Below and opposite: Responding to the increased demand for hearty soups, Campbell began marketing the Manhandler line, the first soups targeted directly at the male members of the average household. After the success of Manhandlers and Stout Hearted Soups, the new chunky line of soups, thick enough to be eaten with a fork,were created to appeal to those who desired substantial, meals-in-themselves soups.

to collect and exhibit eighteenth and nineteenth century soup tureens from around the world, many of which, made from soft-paste porcelain, were extremely fragile and in danger of being lost. (A soup tureen is oval, as opposed to the round bowl traditionally used for stews.) Examples from China, France, Germany, and many other countries, of silver as well as porcelain, were collected, and in 1970 the Campbell Museum opened. The soup tureen collection, the premier of its kind in the world, also traveled to England, Australia, and Japan, as well as to dozens of museums across North America.

Oddly enough, however, some of the Campbell's soups introduced during this period should not properly, if soup etiquette is observed, be served in a tureen. In the late 1960s account executives at BBDO, the ad agency that handled Campbell's soups, noticed that serving soup as a first course at dinner had all but disappeared, especially among middle-class and blue-collar families. They set out to discover why. The BBDO researchers were at first

surprised that, when quizzed about the soup eating habits of their families, housewives usually only mentioned children. When further questioned they explained that soup, along with a sandwich, was a wonderful children's meal, but that it was just too "thin" to be served to their hard-working husbands.

The solution to this problem seemed obvious: market a thick, hearty, filling soup, one that would "stick to the ribs." The advertising executives took the idea to Camden, and together with Campbell personnel they chose thirteen of the thickest soups currently being sold — Bean with Bacon, for instance — and renamed them Manhandlers. An extensive and somewhat revolutionary advertising campaign was planned. For the first time in Campbell's history no women or children were to appear in an ad, only men were to be in Manhandler ads. Frankie Lane was hired to sing the jingle "How do you handle a hungry man? / Manhandlers," and Michael Cimino, a brilliant but at the time generally unknown director, was hired to film the television commercial.

Manhandlers were a huge success, and they begot an even better idea. Why not create a new line of soups that were even thicker and full of more meat and vegetables? What should these soups taste like? How thick should they be? To answer these questions tentatively, a can of Bounty Beef Stew was mixed with a can of Vegetable Soup and heated. What should they be called? Campbell's Fork Soups was the first suggestion. That name was nixed; no soup could be eaten entirely with only a fork. After much discussion

someone suggested Chunky Soups, which was accepted, and in 1969 four were nationally introduced: Chunky Beef, Chunky Chicken, Chunky Vegetable, and Chunky Turkey.

Despite the fact that Chunky Soups were extremely successful, their introduction did not entirely solve the original problem that had led to their creation. For the most part, these soups were eaten as a hot, nutritious, belly-filling lunch rather than as a first course. What many did eat for dinner, however, was another of the company's most successful products at the time: Swanson Hungry-Man Dinners. TV dinners had, of course, been around since the early 1950s, as had the habit of eating them on a tray in front of the television. But the stimulus behind the introduction of these new meals was not just the need for bigger versions of the old TV dinner.

Hungry-Man Dinners, with their larger portions, answered two linked consumer demands. As more and more women entered the work force, it became increasingly difficult for them to prepare the evening meal. Frozen dinners were an obvious solution to this problem. However, as had been the case with soup, homemakers did not consider them as ample as the average home-cooked meal. Hungry-Man Dinners such as Fried Chicken, with its two pieces of meat, and Turkey, with its pile of meat and stuffing, more closely approached the typically copious family dinner, and many rushed and busy families made sure that the freezer compartment was always stocked with a supply.

Hungry-Man Dinners were among the last products introduced during the presidency of W. B. Murphy, an era during which the Campbell Soup

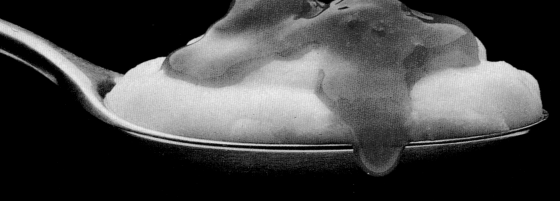

JUST BECAUSE SWANSON STANDS FOR GOOD FOOD, DOESN'T MEAN WE DON'T HAVE A SWEET TOOTH.

This luscious dessert is called cherry cheese creme. It tastes a lot like cheesecake. And to top it off, we've added a layer of juicy cherries.

So now after a well-balanced Swanson meal, you'll get your just desserts

SWANSON DINNERS.

Above: Swanson Hungry-Man
Dinners, with large-size portions of
meat and vegetables plus dessert,
were introduced in 1972.

Company both led and responded to large changes in the eating habits of Americans. In the process, the company had grown enormously. By 1972 earnings were three times what they had been in 1953.

Much of this success was due to the careful stewardship of Dr. Dorrance's son, John, Jr., who since 1962 had held the position of chairman of the board. Known to friends as Jack, he said, "I never thought I had any choice but to work for Campbell," and he spent sixteen years working at various executive levels before assuming the chairmanship. Like his father, Dorrance was publicity-shy; he almost never gave interviews and was seldom photographed. But each day he went to his office in Camden, where few corporate decisions were made without his counsel and judgment.

Beginning in 1972 Campbell's next two presidents, Harold A. Shaub and R. Gordon McGovern, faced a radically changing food environment. Throughout the 1950s and even into the more turbulent 1960s, the old family patterns persisted. To a food company this meant that the father worked and the mother stayed home to manage the household. By the 1970s and 1980s, however, this familiar paradigm was undergoing a structural change. Out of financial necessity more women were entering the work force, which meant that less time was available for food preparation. Convenience was the keynote of home cooking, a fact that made competition in the prepared-food market more intense than ever.

In addition, American families were eating out more often, usually at fast-food restaurants. Campbell attempted to respond to these new demands for convenience in a couple of ways. It continued to introduce more varieties of Hungry-Man Dinners (Chopped Beef Steak and Veal Parmigiana) and Chunky Soups (Split Pea with Ham, Chicken with Rice). For a few years it also entered the restaurant business, acquiring Hanover Trail Steak House and Pietro's Pizza. This foray into running restaurants was short-lived; the company found that its skills were much better suited to consumer goods.

Concurrent with the growing demand for quick, ready-to-serve foods was another, apparently opposing phenomenon, an interest in creative, well-prepared gourmet meals. Unaccountably, the American palate, long known for its predilection for meat, potatoes, and plain, cooked vegetables, learned to appreciate unusual, intense, often international

Above: John T. Dorrance, Jr., son of Dr. John Dorrance, who served as Chairman of the Board of Campbell Soup Company from 1962 until his retirement in 1984. Below: Cream of Mushroom and Golden Mushroom remain among the most popular Campbell's Soups used as a base for gravies and sauces.

flavors. Many people, probably for the first time, became food and cooking enthusiasts, faddists really. As the *New York Times* commented in 1973, "The absolute status symbol of the New York apartment is the kitchen."

In 1977 the newly popular and trendy magazine *Bon Appétit* went even further in reporting the great new enthusiasm for the culinary arts: "These days the food pages of newspapers all over the country list thousands of cooking schools every spring and fall." The magazine continued, "It almost seems as if everybody who ever belonged to the Shallot of the Month Club or owns a butcher-block table or

has some remote ethnic presumption has proclaimed himself dean of his own cooking school."

This "silent revolution of the American palate" could be accurately gauged by the numbers and kinds of cookbooks written during this era. In 1960 only forty-nine cookbooks were published in the United States. By 1972 the number had risen to 385. Cookbook writers were also becoming celebrities of a sort. Star chefs appeared on television preparing classic, complicated, sauce-rich Continental dishes that ten or fifteen years earlier few Americans had heard of, let alone been able to pronounce.

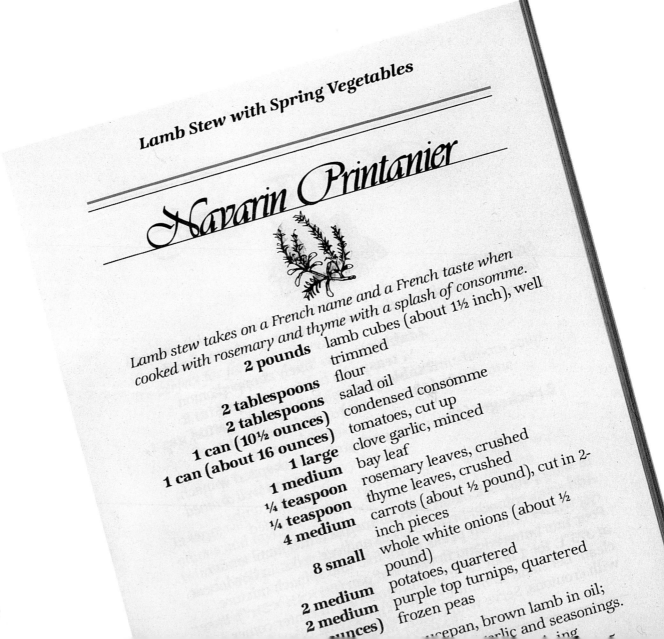

Lamb Stew with Spring Vegetables

Navarin Printanier

Lamb stew takes on a French name and a French taste when cooked with rosemary and thyme with a splash of consomme.

2 pounds	lamb cubes (about 1½ inch), well trimmed
2 tablespoons	flour
2 tablespoons	salad oil
1 can (10½ ounces)	condensed consomme
1 can (about 16 ounces)	tomatoes, cut up
1 large	clove garlic, minced
1 medium	bay leaf
¼ teaspoon	rosemary leaves, crushed
¼ teaspoon	thyme leaves, crushed
4 medium	carrots (about ½ pound), cut in 2-inch pieces
8 small	whole white onions (about ½ pound)
2 medium	potatoes, quartered
2 medium	purple top turnips, quartered
...unces)	frozen peas

...cepan, brown lamb in oil;
...rlic and seasonings.

Lemon Garlic Shrimp

A colorful and surprisingly easy main dish that will impress dinner guests. Pictured opposite.

1 can (14½ ounces) Swanson clear ready to serve chicken broth	1½ pounds medium shrimp, shelled and deveined (about 54)
2 tablespoons cornstarch	¼ cup chopped fresh parsley
2 tablespoons olive oil	2 tablespoons lemon juice
4 cloves garlic, minced	6 cups hot cooked spaghetti
¼ teaspoon grated lemon peel	(12 ounces uncooked)
⅛ teaspoon ground red pepper	Freshly ground black pepper

1. In bowl, stir broth into cornstarch; set aside.

2. In 10-inch skillet over medium heat, in hot oil, cook garlic, lemon peel and red pepper 1 minute, stirring constantly. Add shrimp, parsley and lemon juice. Cook until shrimp are pink, stirring often. Gradually stir in broth mixture. Over medium heat, cook until mixture boils and thickens, stirring constantly. Toss with spaghetti. Serve with freshly ground black pepper. Makes 8 cups or 6 servings.

TO MICROWAVE: Reduce garlic to 3 cloves. In 2-cup glass measure, stir broth into cornstarch. Microwave, uncovered, on HIGH 4 minutes or until mixture boils and thickens, stirring after each minute. Cover; set aside.

In 2-quart microwave-safe casserole, combine oil, 3 cloves garlic, lemon peel and red pepper. Cover with lid; microwave on HIGH 1 minute. Stir in shrimp, parsley and lemon juice. Cover; microwave on HIGH 3 minutes or until most shrimp are pink, stirring once during cooking. Stir in broth mixture. Cover; microwave on HIGH 2 minutes more or until mixture boils and thickens, stirring after each minute. Toss with spaghetti. Serve with freshly ground black pepper.

Fish with Tangy Mustard Sauce

The creamy mustard sauce makes a zesty topper for fish fillets.

1 package (9 ounces) Mrs. Paul's frozen prepared light fillets (haddock or cod)	1 tablespoon spicy brown mustard
½ cup sour cream	6 drops hot pepper sauce

1. Remove create-a-sauce seasoning packet from fish; set aside. Bake fish according to package directions.

2. Meanwhile, in bowl, stir together sour cream, mustard, pepper sauce and contents of create-a-sauce packet. Serve with fish. Makes 2 servings.

Lemon Garlic Shrimp

34

Campbell, which had over the previous thirty years been one of the most prolific publishers of cookbooks, responded quickly to this new culinary climate in America. As the introduction to the 1978 *The Creative Cook* stated:

Cooking is a very personal art. It reflects attitudes and creativity as well as knowledge and skill. In earlier times, cooks were restricted by local harvests and climates, yet the history of cooking is a testament to human ingenuity and adaptation to dynamic changes.

The current American cooking scene, however, is marked by increasingly sophisticated tastes and adventuresome expectations. Our attitudes toward food and cooking are changing with our lifestyles. This cookbook reflects these changes.

In some of its previous cookbooks Campbell had toyed with such dishes as Parmesan Chicken or Meatballs La Scala, but, on the whole, even the names of these entrees were usually Americanized. (On the same page as Skillet Steaks Casino we find Cowpoke Cassoulet, and along with Taco Chicken is Southwest Frankfurters.) Now, however, in cookbooks such as *The International Cook*, dishes were identified by their foreign-language names: the Eastern European Chikhirtma (Tarragon Lamb Soup), the French Carbonades de Boeuf (Beef Braised in Beer), the German Rinderrouladen (Beef Roll-Ups), the Italian Saltimbocca (Chicken Breast with Prosciutto), the Middle Eastern Bamia (Beef and Okra), and the Spanish Pollo en Pepitoria (Saffron

Chicken). In addition to the recipes, short historical introductions to the cuisine of each country were provided, as were glossaries that defined international cooking terms.

Most of these recipes were preceded by headnotes that helped along the budding gourmet cook. Under Miniature Quiches, for instance, which were suggested as appetizers, appeared the following: "Lightly browned crepes are folded into muffin pans. These miniature cups make perfect containers for this excellent quiche filling." Quiche, of course, was at the time not well known, if at all, and the serving of this French delicacy would identify the host or hostess as someone who knew how to prepare elegant food. As usual, the base of the quiche filling is a condensed soup, in this case that ubiquitous white sauce made from Cream of Mushroom.

1 can (10 3/4 ounces) condensed
    Cream of Mushroom soup
1 package (8 ounces) cream cheese,
    softened
4 eggs, slightly beaten
1 cup finely chopped fresh spinach
2/3 cup shredded Swiss cheese
1/2 cup finely chopped ham
1/4 cup finely chopped green onions
1/2 teaspoon hot pepper
24 crepes (6-inch)

Despite its exotic and somewhat novel stature, at least quiche required ingredients that could be found in any kitchen. Not so for many of Campbell's other entrée recipes of the time. Take, for instance, Veal Mediterranean, which is described as "white wine, artichoke hearts, olives, and capers beautifully blended with veal."

1 1/2 pounds veal cubes
2 tablespoons olive oil
1 can (10 3/4 ounces) condensed
    Tomato Soup
1/2 cup Chablis or other dry white wine
1/4 cup water
2 medium cloves garlic, minced
1 package (9 ounces) frozen
    artichoke hearts
2 cups sliced fresh mushrooms
    (about 1/2 pound)
4 slices (about 4 ounces) salami
    cut in strips
1/2 cup pitted ripe olives
2 tablespoons drained capers

Almost half of the ingredients in Veal Mediterranean would, prior to the 1970s, have been unfamiliar to the average American cook. Garlic, for instance, was hardly ever used, and never in this quantity. Few would have cooked with wine, and if they did, they would not have been able to distinguish between varieties. (Wine appreciation also became a passion during the late 1970s and 1980s.) Similarly, artichokes would have been difficult to locate, which is why, presumably, frozen rather than fresh is suggested. And capers — who had ever heard of capers?

The same is generally true of the increasingly liberal use of herbs and

spices. For instance: Albondigas (Spicy Mexican Meatballs) called for crushed oregano leaves; French Lamb Stew for crushed tarragon leaves; Chicken Breasts Espagnole for crushed rosemary leaves; and Coq au Vin for crushed thyme. Though many might have had these herbs in a wall-hung spice rack, they probably had been seldom used and their tastes would have been relatively exotic. (Fresh herbs were generally not included in Campbell's recipes until the 1990s.)

In many ways these recipes were a return, almost full circle, to the sorts of dishes suggested in Campbell's earliest cookbooks. In *Helps for the Hostess*, for example, recipes for elegant and sophisticated entrees such as Stuffed Turbans of Flounder, Potatoes Nanette, Nivernaise Beef, and Spanish Veal Balls were quite common. These kinds of formal dishes, served à *la Russe*, Campbell's cookbooks of the teens considered the "highest test of the social skill and ability of the hostess," those that permitted her to "express her taste and refinement." Now, with a condensed soup as the base of a sauce, they were once again being suggested.

Perhaps the most intriguing aspect of this half-century return to culinary sophistication can be found in those sections of the new Campbell's cookbooks devoted to soups themselves. Many, made with a Campbell's Soup as the base, were classics of international cuisine: Asparagus Leek Soup, for instance, or Italian Escarole Soup or Bouillabaisse. Of the international varieties, two are remarkable for the part they played in the soup history of the company.

PURÉE MONGOLE
A purée is sieved—but you need no strainer for this combination.

1 can (11¼ ounces) condensed green pea soup
1 can (10¾ ounces) condensed tomato soup
1 cup milk
1 cup water

In saucepan, blend soups, milk, and water. Heat; stir. Add a dash of curry powder, if desired. Makes about 4½ cups.

PERK-ME-UP-CUP

½ cup sliced celery
¼ cup chopped green pepper
1 tablespoon butter or margarine
1 can (10½ ounces) condensed beef broth
1 soup can water
2 tablespoons diced pimiento
⅛ teaspoon hot pepper sauce

In saucepan, cook celery and green pepper in butter until tender. Add remaining ingredients. Heat; stir occasionally. Makes about 3½ cups.

MEXICAN FOAM SOUP

¼ cup chopped onion
2 tablespoons chopped green pepper
1 tablespoon butter or margarine
1 can (10½ ounces) condensed tomato soup
1 soup can milk
Generous dash cayenne pepper
1 egg, separated

In saucepan, cook onion and green pepper in butter until tender. Stir in soup, milk, and pepper. Slightly beat egg yolk. Stir a little hot soup mixture into yolk; gradually add to soup. Heat. Beat egg white until very soft peaks form. Add ½ cup soup mixture; beat lightly. Pour on top of soup. Makes about 2½ cups.

Williamsburg Pumpkin Soup Page 164

166

SOUP INDIENNE

2 cans (10 3/4 ounces each)
  condensed Cream of
  Asparagus Soup
1 can (10 3/4 ounces) condensed
  Cream of Celery Soup
1 teaspoon curry powder
2 soup cans water
1 cup chopped apple
1 tablespoon chopped chutney

BEEF BROTH PRINTANIER

2 cans (10 1/2 ounces each)
  condensed Beef Broth
2 soup cans water
1/2 cup thin carrot sticks
  (2-inches long)
1/2 cup thin green pepper strips
  (2-inches long)
1/3 cup diagonally sliced green onions
1/2 cup sliced cherry tomatoes

What is so noteworthy about both of these soup suggestions are neither their ingredients nor their culinary pedigrees (both are classic nineteenth-

◆◆◆

Above: Campbell cookbooks showed that even quite exotic dishes could be prepared using condensed soup as a sauce, although some recipes called for herbs and spices that were not yet familiar to many American home cooks.

FRANCE

As close as the Campbell's Soup on your shelf.

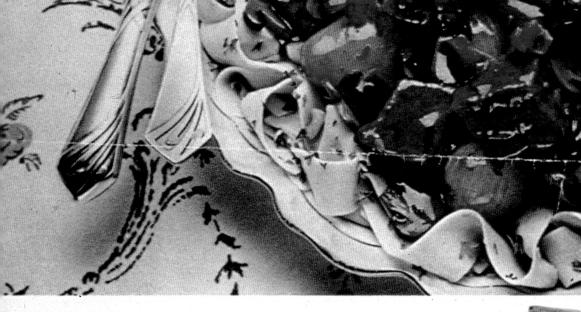

Beef Burgundy

4 slices bacon
1½ pounds beef top round cut
in 1¼-inch cubes
1 can Campbell's Golden
Mushroom Soup
¼ cup burgundy

2 tablespoons chopped parsley
⅛ teaspoon pepper
12 small whole white onions
(about ¾ pound)
2 cups sliced mushrooms
(about ½ pound)

In large saucepan, cook bacon until crisp; remove and crumble.
Brown beef in drippings; pour off fat. Add soup, wine, parsley, and
pepper. Cover; cook over low heat 1 hour 30 minutes. Add onions and
mushrooms; cover and cook 1 hour more or until beef is tender.
Serve over wide noodles. Garnish with bacon and additional parsley.

Cookbook offer: There's a world of good cooking waiting for you in Campbell's "Cooking with Soup" cookbook. Over 600 recipes
fill this beautiful 200-page, hard-covered book. Just send $1.50 and two Campbell's Soup labels with your name, address, and zip code to:
COOKBOOK, Box 1981H, Maple Plain, Minn. 55348. Offer good only in U.S.A. Allow 6 weeks for delivery.

A world of good cooking brought home with Campbell's.

century soups) but the fact that approximately forty years prior to the publication of this particular Campbell cookbook their inclusion would have been unnecessary. Both soups were then readily available, in canned and condensed form, as Campbell's Mulligatawny Soup and Campbell's Printanier Soup. Why had both been discontinued in the late 1930s? Because, quite simply, the American palate was not ready for them; they were too strange and exotic. This is not to say that copious quantities of either were cooked during the great American food renaissance, only that Dr. Dorrance, the creator of the best-selling canned soups in America, was, in easily measurable terms, very much ahead of his time.

If one compares the cookbooks of Dorrance's era to those of the present, the slightly avant-garde nature of his mission is even more apparent. One of the earliest recipes published by the then Joseph Campbell Company was the 1913 Campbell's Tomato Soup with Spaghetti:

Cook 1/2 package spaghetti in boiling salted water twenty minutes, then drain, cover with cold water and drain again. Cut 1/2 lb. bacon in dice, fry, skim out bacon, put in 1 good sized chopped onion and fry golden brown. Add bacon, 1 can Campbell's Tomato Soup and spaghetti and season with salt and pepper to taste. Mix and turn into buttered fireproof dish and bake in moderate oven twenty minutes.

Similar recipes were published in most of the succeeding Campbell cookbooks. (Some, such as Spaghetti Frankfurter Supper, very much reflect the distinctly nonethnic tastes of the times.) Campbell also continued to manufacture the very popular Franco-American canned spaghetti, but that had become predominantly a child's food. (Spaghetti O's were created to help the child who had trouble with the strands spoon up the dish.) By the 1970s, however, with the increased interest in international and ethnic foods, spaghetti, renamed "pasta," had become common on the American table. This does not imply that most

INTERNATIONAL VIA CAMPBELL'S SOUP.

It's a new party idea.

Plain old hamburger starts talking with a delicious foreign accent when you sauce it up with Campbell's Soup. See opposite page for the how-to.

"My daughter-in-law just beat my pot roast.
With Campbell's Soup no less."

"I'm going to send for
the recipe book and
see what else is new."

It takes a good cook to know one.
And good cooks know that Campbell's
Soups add extra flavor and richness to
everything—from pot roasts to vegetables, gravies to desserts.
Try the recipes here. Then send
for the cookbook for more. (Why not get
an extra one for your mother-in-law!)

PERFECT POT ROAST (Makes 6 to 8 servings)

3 to 4-pound boneless pot roast
1 can Campbell's Beef Broth
½ teaspoon salt
¼ teaspoon pepper
¼ teaspoon rosemary leaves, crushed (optional)
6 small carrots, cut in half lengthwise (about ½ pound)
2 medium yellow turnips, quartered (about 1½ pounds)
8 small whole white onions (about ½ pound)

1. In large heavy pan, brown meat on all sides (use shortening if necessary); pour off fat.
2. Add soup and seasonings.
3. Cover; cook over low heat 2 hours.
4. Add carrots, turnips, and onions.
5. Cook 1 hour more or until done.
6. Stir occasionally.
7. Remove meat and vegetables to heated platter.
8. Spoon off fat; thicken to desired consistency.
9. Garnish with parsley if desired.
Menu suggestion: Serve with biscuits, cucum-ber and tomato salad with Italian dressing and vanilla pudding with cookies for dessert.

BEST-EVER MEAT LOAF (Makes 6 to 8 servings)

1 can (10¾ ounces) Campbell's Tomato, Golden Mushroom, or Cream of Mushroom Soup
2 pounds ground beef
½ cup fine dry bread crumbs
⅓ cup finely chopped onion
1 egg, slightly beaten
1 teaspoon salt
2 tablespoons water

1. Mix thoroughly ½ cup soup, beef, bread crumbs, onion, egg, and salt.
2. Shape firmly into loaf (8x4"); place in shallow baking pan.
3. Bake at 375°F. for 1 hour and 15 minutes.
4. Blend remaining soup, water, and 2 to 3 table-spoons drippings.
5. Heat; stir occasionally; serve with loaf.
Menu suggestion: Serve with baked potatoes, green beans and apple pie for dessert.

Cookbook Offer: Get more than 600 excit-ing recipes in Campbell's "Cooking with Soup" Cookbook. Send $1.50 and any two Campbell's Soup labels with your name, address and zip code to COOKBOOK, BOX 494, Maple Plain, Minn. 55348. Offer good only in U.S.A. May be withdrawn at any time. Void where prohibited or restricted. Allow six weeks for delivery.

Give me the
Campbell Life.

Above: Campbell's Tomato Soup
and Beef Broth advertisement,
from 1976. Opposite: The increased emphasis on slimming,
healthy foods in the American
diet beginning in the 1970s led
to "soup and salad" becoming
a popular lunch, an idea that
Campbell enthusiastically promoted.

American cooks made their own
sauces; they clearly did not; they used
prepared sauces. In 1981 Campbell,
under the Prego label, introduced its
own spaghetti sauces, a product line
that became one of the company's
most successful of the time.

The American food renaissance
had another important effect on
Campbell's product lines. Again, this
was the result of the intersection of
two unrelated trends. The public's
appetite for fresh, flavorful, well-
seasoned dishes often conflicted with
its desire for food that could be

prepared in a hurry. The intersection
of these two desires led to the introduction of Le Menu frozen dinners: well-
seasoned, well-prepared meals that
could be heated and served in minutes.
(Some 368 names, such as American
Classics and Chef's Selections, were
considered, but Le Menu was chosen
because it sounded French but was
not so French that it was difficult to
pronounce.)

Along with all these changes in
American eating habits also came a
concurrent interest in light and
nutritious foods. Lightness was an
offshoot of the new interest in haute
cuisine. Many of the international
recipes that were in vogue in the early
period of the American food renaissance, especially those that were
French, were rich, sauce-heavy, and
laden with calories. As elegant as they
were, they were sometimes also
perceived as fattening and unhealthy.

In response to this, a new wave
of French chefs created a "nouvelle
cuisine," a revolutionary way of cooking
that considered diet and health along
with taste, freshness, and length of
cooking time. (Sometimes the nouvelle
cuisine menus were merely trendy —
light, almost airy, with quaint and
bizarrely unconventional ingredients.
Among the dishes offered on food
writer Mindy Heiferling's "Nouvelle
Hell" menu were Sea Urchin Roe with
Goat Cheese, Poached Monkfish
Cheeks with Fresh Ginger Mayonnaise,
and Mesquite-Broiled Crème Brûlée!)

One of these nouvelle chefs, Michel
Guérard, titled his cookbook *Cuisine
Minceur*, the cuisine of slimness, a
promise that went hand in hand with
the other great concern of the time,

SALADS

Delicious and economical dressings are as close as the Campbell's Soups on your shelf.

Mushroom Dressing

1 can Campbell's Cream
   of Mushroom Soup
¼ cup water
¼ cup tarragon vinegar
1½ tablespoons sugar
1 teaspoon dry mustard
¼ teaspoon celery seed
¼ teaspoon marjoram
   leaves, crushed
Dash Worcestershire

In saucepan, combine
ingredients. Heat; stir
occasionally. Chill. Serve
with spinach salad.
Makes about 1½ cups.

Italian Cheese Dressing

1 can (10¾ ounces)
   Campbell's Tomato Soup
½ cup salad or olive oil
¼ cup vinegar
¼ cup grated Parmesan
   cheese
1 teaspoon basil leaves
1 teaspoon oregano leaves
⅛ teaspoon garlic salt

In covered jar or shaker,
combine ingredients;
chill. Shake well before
using. Serve with tossed
green salad. Makes
about 2 cups.

Zesty French Dressing

1 can (10¾ ounces)
   Campbell's Tomato Soup
½·cup salad oil
¼ cup vinegar
2 tablespoons sugar
1 tablespoon finely
   chopped onion
2 teaspoons dry mustard
1 teaspoon salt
¼ teaspoon pepper

In covered jar or shaker, combine ingredients; chill. Shake
well before using. Serve with
chef's salad or salad greens.
Makes about 2 cups.

A world of good salad dressings brought home with Campbell's.

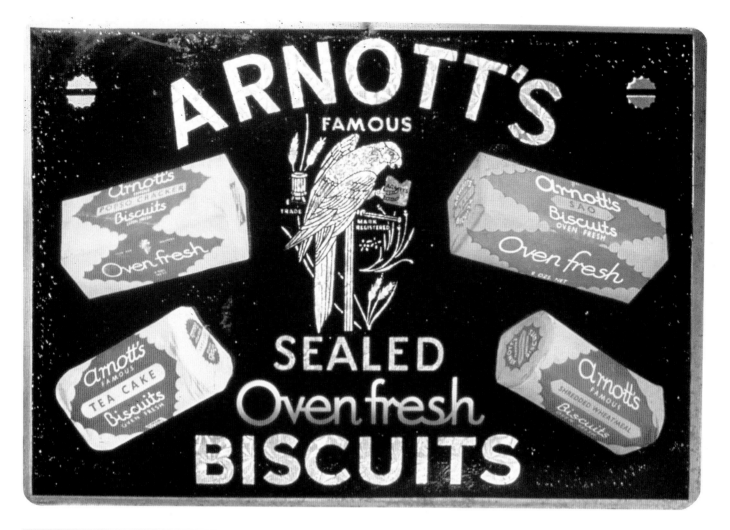

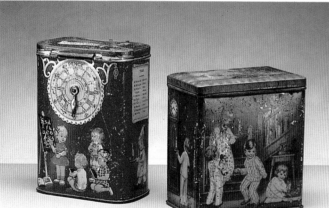

Above: In 1993 Campbell's acquired a majority interest in Arnott's, a 125-year-old Australian biscuit company.

nutritional value. Food was judged not only by its lack of caloric richness but also by its low fat content and wealth of vitamins, minerals, and protein. Campbell responded to the new demand for light, nutritional foods in a numbers of ways. Soups had always been considered wholesome, but the company introduced two new varieties: low-sodium soups for those on restricted diets and Healthy Request ready-to-serve and condensed soups, with one-third less salt and less fat than traditional soups. Campbell also introduced its own versions of *cuisine minceur*: Le Menu Lightstyle Entrees. Pepperidge Farm followed this trend with Wholesome Choice cookies and crackers.

The new era was a rather wild time in the prepared-food industry. Under the presidencies of Shaub and McGovern, Campbell introduced nearly four hundred new products. Some, such as Prego, were huge successes. Others, like Pepperidge Farm Star Wars Cookies and Juice Works (children's juices packed in bottles and cans), for example, proved only meteoric. (Pepperidge Farm cookies were generally not considered kids' products, and juice in disposable cardboard boxes was the rage of the moment.) The company continued to grow in other areas of the food business as well, acquiring such well-known brands as Vlasic Pickles and Olives, Marie's Salad Dressings, and Open Pit Barbecue Sauce, among others.

Campbell also began to turn its attention overseas. Since the 1930s the company had made efforts to open new international markets, and oper-

ations were begun in Canada (1930), England (1933), Mexico (1959), and Australia (1961). This trend continued when, under David W. Johnson, Campbell's eighth president, the company acquired a majority interest in Arnott's, the largest and oldest commercial bakery in Australia. Arnott's ranked in some ways as the Campbell of Australia, and its acquisition was very much in line with Campbell's historical growth strategy.

As previously mentioned, during the 1970s and 1980s Campbell had been led by Harold A. Shaub and then R. Gordon McGovern, both of whom had risen through the corporate ranks. Under Shaub the company had

Below: In tune with the times Vlasic pickle chunks were advertised as low in calories, but still delicious.

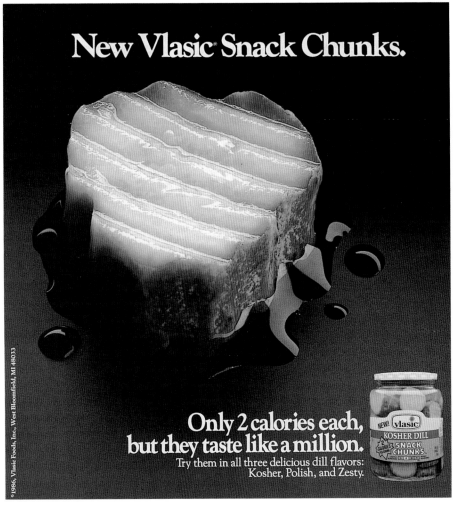

°1986, Vlasic Foods, Inc., West Bloomfield, MI 48033

Below and opposite: The well-known Campbell's soups are found all around the globe, for example in China, Mexico, Canada, Japan, the United Kingdom, and Argentina.

continued to emphasize gains in production know-how and product improvement. McGovern, however, thought changes were in order. In an effort to increase sales, the company introduced nearly five hundred new products during the eighties, many of which were dramatic successes.

McGovern also saw the importance of the global marketplace. "I knew," he said of the time, "that if we didn't have a strategy to compete worldwide, we'd have a tough time growing in the years ahead." Sometimes, of course, the achievement of this goal was not as easy as it sounded. After many years of effort in Japan, for instance, sales of V8 juice had only shown fair acceptance. Only when Campbell teamed up with a Japanese partner, Suntory, would V8 sales find vigor.

Campbell earnings through the 1980s turned sluggish, and Australian-born David W. Johnson was tapped in January 1990 as president and CEO of the company. Giving the nod to the power of Campbell's brands, especially its line of soups, Johnson was greeted

by three trumpeters playing a chorus, of "Mm! Mm! Good!" as the new president and his wife first entered the company's corporate offices in Camden. (He later showed up at a meeting of top executives wearing the red cape of Souperman.)

Johnson was the first outsider to lead the company, but he came with impressive credentials as a "business warrior" with worldwide experience: president, American Chicle Division, Warner Lambert; president and CEO, Entenmann's, Inc.; president, chairman, and CEO, Gerber Products Company. "As a young man in Australia, I knew that running a major American company would be my life's goal," said Johnson. "Being named CEO of Campbell was the fulfillment of that dream."

He went to work immediately. Johnson renewed the company's drive for performance. He consolidated plants, including the original Camden factory, and streamlined many operations by eliminating nonessential jobs. He created a North American division that included the United States, Canada, and Mexico in the belief that this trading group was inevitable. "This is the way it has to be," he said, "if we are to compete against the European Common Market and the tigers of Asia." The acquisition of majority interest in Arnotts was intended to add additional ammunition to Campbell's Asian effort, which pointed to the marketing of soup in mainland China, whose citizens consume more soup per capita every few weeks than Americans do in a year. "If you're in the soup business, you have to be in China," said Johnson.

The Souper Dress.

It's a pretty groovy deal just for enjoying Campbell's Vegetable Soup.

Now's your chance to get the one, the only *Souper Dress* . . . a smashing paper put-on that could only come from Campbell. It's got eye-poppin' Campbell's cans coming and going! And it's all yours for eating your vegetables . . . your Campbell's Vegetable Soups, that is. You can choose from: Campbell's Old-Fashioned Vegetable, Vegetable Beef, Chicken Vegetable, Vegetarian Vegetable and Turkey Vegetable, as well as good old Campbell's Vegetable Soup.

To get your Campbell Paper Dress, send the labels from any 2 different kinds of Campbell's Vegetable Soups, $1.00 and your size (the *Souper Dress* comes Small/5-8, Medium/9-12, or Large/13-16) with your name and address (remember your zip code!) to Dress Offer, Box 560, Maple Plain, Minn. 55359. Offer expires Mar. 31, 1968. Good only in the United States and Puerto Rico.*
Campbell's *Souper Dress*. On you, it'll look . . .

M'm! M'm! Good!

*Void if taxed, restricted or forbidden by law.

Above and opposite: Licensed and promotional items related to Campbell products and logos earned the company additional income, but as much as anything served as adjunct advertising to spread the name more widely.

By the early 1990s Campbell was grossing over $6 billion dollars in overall sales, a remarkable number considering that the year Dr. Dorrance entered its employ the Joseph Campbell Preserve Company lost $60,000. No longer just an American soup company, Campbell now had over twenty-five subsidiaries and affiliates. From one small plant on the Camden waterfront its manufacturing operations now numbered close to ninety all over the world. And, under the leadership of its latest president, the company was aggressively seeking to take its place in the new global economy.

The Campbell name had become, as Warhol had suggested, an icon of sorts. The phrase "the familiar red-and-white can" had only one meaning: Campbell's Soup. This place in the culinary sensibility was, no doubt, achieved by a measured and sometimes conservative pace of growth. As food historian Irena Chalmers described this business strategy:

Mass appeal depends on the existence of look-alike tastes. So what do you do? You pour products into the market that match these tastes, products you're able to manufacture economically and also have stored in abundance in distribution centers all around the globe. You expand the list by acquiring companies that make similar products. And you run such a mass business best through a highly centralized organizational structure.

This description generally fits the historical operations of the Campbell Soup Company. But Chalmers's shorthand account of the company's success formula is probably even better: "Product plus package equals quality." To this, of course, must be added the qualifying phrase "over time." To succeed in settling itself solidly into the daily lives of millions of people, a food company such as Campbell must produce prepared foods whose labels instantly imply reliable high quality. And a company such as Campbell must continue to do this year after year across wide geography and a great array of products.

One of the most graphic examples of the historical truth of this principle can be found in the list of the top-ten-selling Campbell's soups of 1992.

These rank, along with the dates of their introduction: (1) Chicken Noodle-1934, (2) Cream of Mushroom-1934, (3) Tomato-1897, (4) Cream of Chicken-1947, (5) Vegetable Beef-1918, (6) Chicken with Rice-1913, (7) Cream of Broccoli-1990, (8) Vegetable-1899, (9) Cream of Celery-1913, (10) Vegetarian Vegetable-1937. Given the ever-changing tastes of the public, the difficulties of manufacturing and marketing, and the length of time the company has been in business, this is a remarkable list.

Two of the top ten, Tomato and Vegetable, have been around almost a hundred years. Tomato, of course, owes its standing to the fact that for a good deal of its history it has served as both a cooking and an eating soup. Vegetable, on the other hand, is, along with chicken soup, practically a simulacrum of soup as a hot, nutritious, health-giving food.

Among the three soups first introduced around World War I, Vegetable Beef was specifically created to provide soldiers on the European front with

Above and below: Cream of Broccoli, introduced in 1990, was the first new soup to enter the list of Campbell's top ten best-selling since Cream of Chicken in 1947. Along with Broccoli Cheese, introduced in 1991, Cream of Broccoli is often used as a cooking soup.

a convenient, super-nutritious meal. It shares with Chicken with Rice the image of "down-home" cooking, the sort of soup that is psychologically comforting. The odd one in this group is Cream of Celery, which was originally offered as a thick, smooth puree but has since become primarily a cooking soup.

Two of the three soups of the 1930s are pivotal in the Campbell history. Chicken, of course, is the most popular soup of all time, whether prepared at home or in a restaurant or purchased in a can. Even more than Vegetable, it is valued not only for its smooth taste, but for its reputation as a restorative, the broth one drinks to feel better. Add noodles to this soup as a filling garnish, and it is no wonder

that Chicken Noodle is the best-selling Campbell's soup. Almost since its introduction in 1934, Cream of Mushroom has been the epitome of a cooking soup. (While 80 percent is used as an ingredient, the remaining 20 percent that is enjoyed as soup would, by itself, place Cream of Mushroom in the top ten.)

Though the idea of soup as sauce was advertised early in the company's history, not until the creation of Cream of Mushroom did it completely take hold in the mind of the average buyer of Campbell's products. Once it did, of course, there followed a massive change in the style of foods eaten by the average American family. In fact, it is probably fair to suggest that the use of sauces in cooking at least in part prepared the way for a general rise in the sophistication of American cookery, a goal that had been part of Dr. John Dorrance's general strategy in 1897.

Cream of Chicken, the first post–World War II soup on the list, is also primarily a cooking soup, as is Cream of Broccoli, the single contemporary soup to break into the top ten. At first the latter soup was marketed as a high-quality eating soup, but sales were only mediocre. Then research showed that it was used mostly in cooking. The product was reformulated, and an extensive campaign, complete with a "Get President George Bush to Eat Broccoli" recipe contest, was launched.

One of the most remarkable things about Cream of Broccoli was to be found on its label. The medallion that had been the centerpiece of the Campbell's label for almost 120 years

Two Great Ways To Make Broccoli A Part Of Your Dinner.

Mm! Mm! Good!

was replaced by a full-color picture of a bunch of broccoli. Had Campbell's icon, the red-and-white design memorialized by Andy Warhol, outlived its usefulness? Not at all. Most Campbell's Soups still looked like the Warhol print. Did the change confuse customers? Again, not at all. Cream of Broccoli was the first new soup since 1947 to enter the top ten. Would this label change signal a radical shift in the image of Campbell's products? Unlikely.

Will a twenty-first-century Warhol, replicating the look of Campbell's products, be faced with a greater diversity of images? Probably. Will, however, the universality of the Campbell brand provide this Warhol of the future with an equal wealth of memory-provoking material? Almost certainly.

Below: The ubiquitous image of the Campbell soup can found its way to Hollywood in 1993, when noted film director Billy Wilder collaborated with artist Bruce Houston to create this sculpture which was exhibited at the Louis Stern Gallery in Beverly Hills.

Andy Warhol and The Campbell Images

PAGE 188

Campbell's Soup Can and Dollar Bills. 1962. Pencil and watercolor on paper, 24 x 18". Collection Roy and Dorothy Lichtenstein, New York.

PAGE 189

Campbell's Soup Can (Tomato). 1965. Synthetic polymer paint and silkscreen ink on canvas, 36 1/4 x 24 1/4". The Menil Collection, Houston.

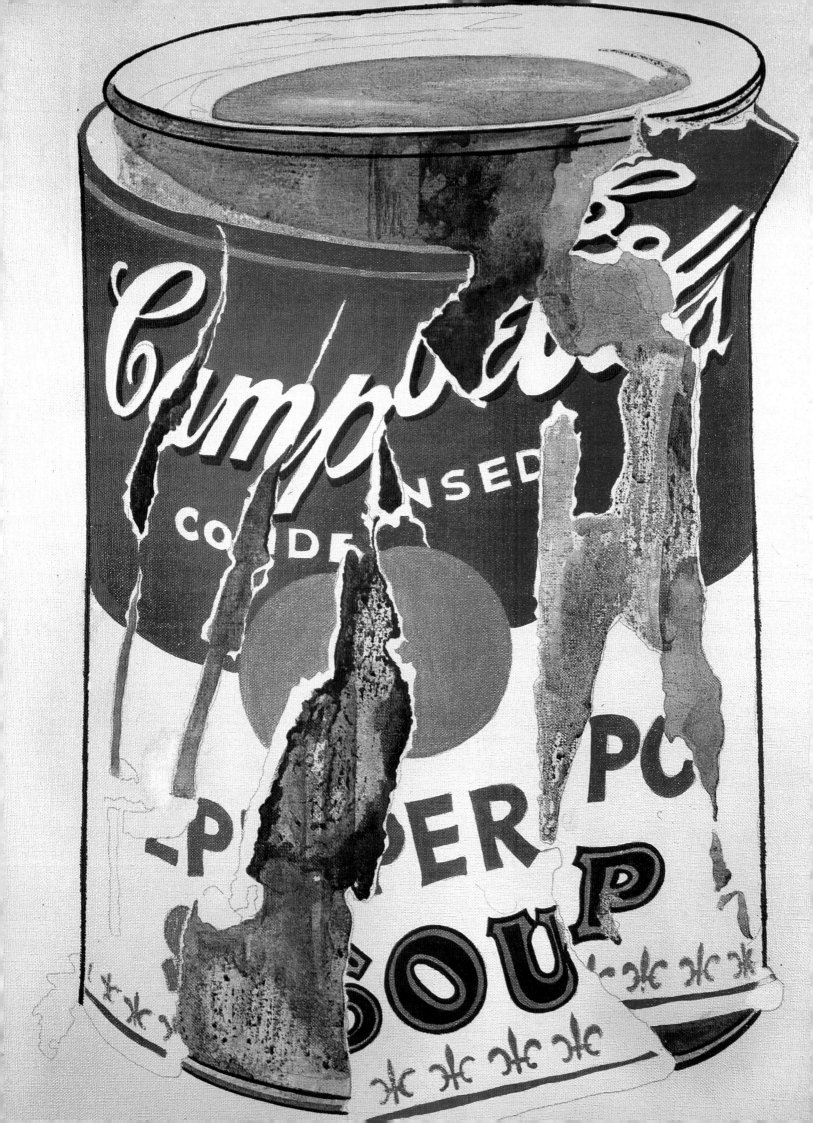

PAGE 190

*Campbell's Soup Can
(Pepper Pot, Peeling Label).*
1962. Synthetic polymer
paint on canvas, 20 x 16".
Collection Irving Blum,
New York.

PAGE 191 TOP

*Big Torn Campbell's
Soup Can (Pepper Pot).*
1962. Synthetic polymer
paint and Prestype on
canvas, 71 3/4 x 51 3/4".
The Andy Warhol
Museum Founding
Collection, Contribution
The Andy Warhol
Foundation for the
Visual Arts, Inc.

PAGE 191 LEFT

Campbell's Soup Can 19¢.
1962. Synthetic polymer
paint and pencil on
canvas, 72 x 54 1/2".
The Menil Collection,
Houston.

PAGE 191 RIGHT

*Crushed Campbell's Soup
Can (beef Noodle).* 1962.
Synthetic polymer
paint and pencil on
canvas, 72 x 52".The
Andy Warhol Museum
Founding Collection,
Contribution The Andy
Warhol Foundation
for the Visual Arts, Inc.

PAGE 193
Studio view — The
Factory, New York City.
c. 1964. Photograph
courtesy Archives
Malanga.

PAGES 194–195
*200 Campbell's Soup
Cans.* 1962. Synthetic
polymer paint on
canvas, 72 x 100".
Private collection.
Photograph courtesy
Leo Castelli Gallery,
New York.

PAGE 196
Campbell's Soup. 1965.
Oil on canvas, 36 x 24".
Private collection.

PAGE 197 LEFT
*Colored Campbell's
Soup (Tomato).* 1965.
(Green background)
Silkscreen ink on
synthetic polymer paint
on canvas, 36 x 24".
Private collection.

PAGE 197 RIGHT
*Colored Campbell's
Soup (Tomato).* 1965.
(Blue background)
Silkscreen ink on
synthetic polymer paint
on canvas, 36 x 24".
Private collection.

PAGE 198 TOP
Campbell's Noodle Soup Box. Campbell's Onion Mushroom Box. Campbell's Chicken Noodle Box. 1986. All: synthetic polymer paint and silkscreen ink on canvas, 20 x 20".

PAGE 198 BOTTOM
Silkscreen on shopping bag. c. 1966. Designed by Andy Warhol.

Epilogue

No great thing is created suddenly, any more than a bunch of grapes or a fig. If you tell me that you desire a fig, I answer that there must be time. Let it first blossom, then bear the fruit, then ripen.

— Epictetus

By its 125th year, 1994, Campbell Soup Company had blossomed into one of America's great corporations. With its products in virtually every home, its trademark red-and-white can an American icon, and its name among the most established in the United States, Campbell had become truly an American institution.

By its 125th year Campbell had grown from a national provider of soup to an international food-processing source of strength. Its 47,000 employees at some one hundred facilities in more than a dozen countries produced thousands of different products marketed on six continents.

By its 125th year Campbell had more #1 and #2 brands per dollar of sales than any other food company in the United States, with some of the finest brands existing anywhere: *Campbell's... Pepperidge Farm...Vlasic... Swanson... Mrs. Paul's... Prego... Godiva... Marie's...Franco-American,* and others around the world... *Kattus...Fray Bentos...Devos Lemmens...Delacre... Arnott's...*

By its 125th year Campbell's flagship soup business enjoyed its role as the steadfast leader in the company's business portfolio: "Soup is our middle name."

Today Americans purchase almost 2.5 billion cans of Campbell's Soup each year, which means that more than seventy cans are sold every second.

Campbell soups are purchased more often than any other product in supermarkets nationally. Three of the six top selling grocery items in 1994 were Campbell's Chicken Noodle, Cream of Mushroom, and Tomato Soups.

Above and right: Among many
recent activities on behalf of the
communities where Campbell
people live and work was a major
Campbell underwriting of a new
aquarium in Camden, New Jersey.
Here, children and adults alike
learn more about life in Delaware
Valley waters.

Success of some of Campbell's community outreach programs include a variety of activities and services, from inner-city child care programs to literacy promotion. One program, called "Labels for Education" has, for more than twenty years, supplied primary and secondary schools and libraries in many communities with educational equipment, ranging from computers, projectors, and microscopes to transportation vehicles.

For preparing recipes, Campbell's Soup ranks in the four most popular ingredients used in America.

Soup is in more American households than eggs, ready-to-serve cereal, pasta, sugar, paper towels, rice, coffee, and colas — even bathroom tissue.

If John T. Dorrance and his immediate successors focused on building a company, later CEOs extended its reach by energizing its various elements: Harold A. Shaub in the 1970s guided Campbell to industry-leading manufacturing prowess; R. Gordon McGovern gave life to marketing and new products during the fast-paced 1980s; and in the 1990s, Australia-born David W. Johnson ushered in a new era, with clear aim at global presence and international brand superiority. "Campbell Brands Preferred Around the World" became the company's vision — to be achieved through employees joined in a crusade to seize the future.

Johnson, who, before joining Campbell, had led major businesses on four continents, found himself in much the same position as Dr. Dorrance in the early days of Campbell. Just as Dorrance had set out to build a consumer business by introducing his condensed and canned soups to a nation that had known only the homemade kind, Johnson faced the same challenge when he launched Campbell's Soup in China and other countries where the concept of prepared soup was unknown. Just as Dorrance had to build the infrastructure to get soup on store shelves across the country, Johnson had to extend that infrastructure to faraway ports. To the anthem "Carpe Futurum!" Campbell management began to build a diverse, talented team from around

the world. To increase its stable of powerful brands, a new and rich force of brainpower would have to be unleashed.

Just as Dr. Dorrance had led the effort to develop state-of-the-art manufacturing in his day, so the company's engineers and scientists in the 1990s face new sciences and more complex technologies. Examples abound: flexible manufacturing lines, flavor sciences, quality assurance programs, computer-based business systems and others.

Dr. Dorrance answered the daunting challenge by building a national company that would prosper in the twentieth century; Johnson's aspiration is to build a global company that will prosper in the twenty-first. And so, in Campbell's 125th year, the process begins anew. Campbell once again stands on the threshold of a new century with opportunities no less rousing than those that challenged Dr. Dorrance in the early 1900s.

As Johnson has stated: "A company can live forever. The ultimate challenge for each succeeding leadership is to protect the company's heritage while responding to and creating change. The final determinant is superior performance in building long-term shareowner wealth."

A timeless philosophy, one that Dr. Dorrance himself would embrace.

Campbell Soup Company

Chronology

Campbell Soup Company

Joseph Campbell   *Abraham Anderson*

1860 **1870**

1869

Joseph Campbell, a fruit merchant, and
Abraham Anderson, an icebox manufacturer,
form partnership to can tomatoes, vegetables,
jellies, condiments, and mincemeat. First
plant in Camden, New Jersey.

1876

Anderson leaves partnership; Arthur Dorrance
and Joseph Campbell form new company.

1880	1890	1900

1891

Company name changes to Joseph Campbell Preserve Company; incorporated in New Jersey ten years later.

1894

Arthur Dorrance succeeds Joseph Campbell as President; Campbell retires and dies in 1900, ending association of Campbell family with the company.

1895

Joseph Campbell Preserve Company markets a ready-to-serve beefsteak tomato soup.

1897

Arthur Dorrance reluctantly agrees to hire his 24-year-old nephew, Dr. John T. Dorrance, as company chemist at a token wage of just $7.50 a week. Dr. Dorrance develops formula for condensed soups.

1898

A company executive attends annual Cornell-Penn football game and is so taken with Cornell's brilliant new red and white uniforms he convinces Campbell to use the colors on soup labels.

1899

First advertising on New York City streetcars.

1900

Campbell's soups win Gold Medallion for excellence at Paris Exposition; medallion featured on labels.

1904

Campbell's Pork & Beans introduced. Campbell Kids are "born" when a Philadelphia artist sketches them for a series of streetcar advertisements.

1905

First magazine advertisement in *Good Housekeeping* notes: "21 Kinds of Campbell's Soup — 16 million cans sold in 1904."

Dr. John T. Dorrance

Arthur C. Dorrance

1910   **1920**   **1930**

1911
Campbell's soups achieve national
distribution.

1914
Dr. John T. Dorrance assumes presidency
of the company.

1915
Campbell acquires Franco-American Food
Company, maker of gourmet foods.

1916
Idea of cooking with condensed soup introduced in first Campbell cookbook, *Helps for
the Hostess.* Today, more than one million cans
of soup are used *every day* in recipes in the
United States.

1922
America loves condensed soups so much,
Campbell adopts "soup" as its middle name,
officially changing company name to
Campbell Soup Company.

1930
Dr. John T. Dorrance dies and is succeeded as
President by his brother, Arthur C. Dorrance.
Canadian subsidiary is organized.

1934
Campbell's Chicken Noodle and Cream of
Mushroom soups introduced.

1937
Margaret Rudkin, a Fairfield, Connecticut,
wife and mother, founds Pepperidge Farm,
Incorporated.

James McGowan, Jr.

William B. Murphy

1940   **1950**   **1960**

1942
Sales top $100 million mark.

1945
American businessman Joseph Vlasic
begins marketing Polish-style pickles under
the *Vlasic* label.

1946
Arthur C. Dorrance dies and is succeeded
as President by James McGowan, Jr. Mrs.
Paul's Kitchens is founded in Philadelphia.

1948
V8 vegetable juice is acquired.

1950s
In the basement of Marie's Cafe in Seattle,
Washington, Harold Smith creates *Marie's*
blue cheese salad dressing.

1951
Swanson chicken, turkey and beef pot pies
introduced.

1953
James McGowan, Jr. retires and William B.
Murphy is elected President. Campbell Soup
Fund is organized as a private grantmaking,
non-profit corporation to direct funds to
non-profit organizations in the U.S.

1954
Campbell goes public with common stock and
is admitted to trading on the New York Stock
Exchange.

1955
Campbell acquires C. A. Swanson & Sons,
originators of the *TV Dinner.*

1957
New corporate headquarters opens in Camden,
New Jersey. Company establishes International
Division.

1958
Sales exceeded $500 million. Campbell
enters continental Europe.

1959
Campbell's de Mexico, S.A. de C.V., and
Campbell's Soups (Australia) Pty. Limited are
formed. New plant opens at King's Lynn,
England.

1961
Campbell acquires Pepperidge Farm bakery
products manufacturer and Biscuits Delacre,
Belgian cookie and confection maker.

1962
Pop artist Andy Warhol paints first *Campbell's*
soup cans. When asked why, he once said,
"Because I used to drink (soup). I used to have
the same lunch every day for 20 years."

1965
Food Service Division is created.
Franco-American SpaghettiOs introduced.

1966
Campbell acquires Godiva Chocolatier, Inc.,
quality candy manufacturer.

Harold A. Shaub

R. Gordon McGovern

David W. Johnson

1970　　　　　　　　　　**1980**　　　　　　　　　　**1990**

1970
Campbell's Chunky ready-to-serve soups introduced. Campbell Museum opens in Camden as a showcase for outstanding soup tureen collections.

1971
Sales top $1 billion.

1972
William B. Murphy retires; succeeded as president by Harold A. Shaub.

1973
Campbell introduces *Labels for Education* program nationally.

1978
Vlasic Foods, Inc., is acquired.

1972
Sales top $2 billion.

1980
R. Gordon McGovern succeeds Harold A. Shaub as President. Swift-Armour S.A. Argentina is acquired.

1981
Prego spaghetti sauces introduced nationally.

1982
Mrs. Paul's Kitchens, Inc. is acquired.

1983
Sales top $3 billion.

1985
Campbell commissions Andy Warhol to paint *Campbell's* soup box.

1986
The *Swanson* aluminum frozen dinner tray takes a place in the Smithsonian Museum of American History when microwavable plastic trays are introduced.

1987
Sales top $4 billion. Campbell acquires *Open Pit* barbecue sauce retail line.

1988
Campbell acquires *Marie's* refrigerated salad dressings and *Early California* and *Durkee* olives.

1989
John T. Dorrance, Jr., former Chairman of the Board and son of the originator of condensed soups, dies.

1990
David W. Johnson assumes presidency.

1991
Sales top $6 billion. Campbell acquires *Sanwa* ramen noodle soups.

1992
Corporate vision "Campbell Brands Preferred Around the World" adopted. Campbell launches soups in China, Poland, and Argentina. First international cookbook, *Simply Delicious Recipes*, published in French, Spanish and English, bringing idea of cooking-with-soup to consumers worldwide.

1993
Campbell wins majority interest in Arnotts Ltd. (Australia), the seventh largest biscuit manufacturer in the world. Campbell acquires *Fray Bentos*, the United Kingdom's leading brand in premium canned meats. Campbell and Nakano Vinegar Co. Ltd. create joint venture to market *Campbell's* soups in Japan. David W. Johnson is elected to additional post of Chairman. A newly created position of Vice Chairman is filled by Bennett Dorrance.

1994
Campbell celebrates 125th anniversary.

Acknowledgments

For help in researching the historical material included in this publication thanks are due to a number of people at Campbell Soup Company: J. Neil Stalter, Vice-President, Public Affairs, who brought this project to Abrams and who oversaw its completion; Pat Teberg, Corporate Editor, Publishing, and her colleague Alice Carter, who managed the enormous paper flow and served as valuable liaisons to Abrams; Campbell Archivist Jan Dickler, without whose good taste, judgment, and good cheer this would have been a different book; Ralph Collier, President, Campbell Museum; Group Director of Public Relations, Jim Moran, who often steered me in the right directions; and Carol Ritchie, Manager/Promotions, always ready to help in the search for visual material.

Among Campbell retirees three were especially helpful: former President William Beverly Murphy, a man of wide knowledge of the company's middle period; and Bud Denton and Scott Rombach, careful readers of the historical manuscript. Additionally, much appreciation goes to Mrs. Samuel Hamilton, who provided valuable genealogical information about the Dorrance family tree and who generously made available visual material in her collection.

At Harry N. Abrams, Mark Greenberg and Robert Morton deserve special thanks, Mark for his initial management of the project and Bob for his final editing of the historical text, captions, and illustrations.

Index

A & P Company, 86
A. C. Nielsen Company, 128
acquisition philosophy of
    Campbell Soup Company, 154
advertising, 87–90
    See also Campbell Kids; marketing; *specific products*
    agencies, 44, 147, 150, 168
    aimed at consumer and grocer, *40, 41, 42, 43*
    "Amos 'n' Andy", *120–21*
    booklets, *46*, 53
    budget, 97
    of Campbell products, *135, 136*
    "Campbell's Soup position", 89
    ceramic mincemeat bowl, *26*
    Charlie Chaplin cartoon, *41*
    cookbooks in, *63*, 121
    creating goodwill, 145, 147
    dolls, *48*, 50, *52, 53, 68, 69, 148*
    early days, *38, 39*
    early-twentieth-century, 98, 100
    grocery store window layouts, *51*
    history of, 44–53
    jingles, 49–50, 97, 150, 168
    and Joseph Campbell Preserve Company, 44
    for ketchup, *23, 24*
    labels of Joseph Campbell and Company, *20, 21*
    labels of Joseph Campbell Preserve Company, *28*
    licensed collectible products, *184, 185*
    magazine color ads, *91*
    newspapers and magazines, 50, 53, 89–90, 206
    original color and design for soup label, *27, 37*
    policy of Arthur C. Dorrance, 121–22
    postcards, 50, *64, 65*
    promotional products, *26*, 50, *109, 150, 184, 185*
    radio, 122, 124
    streetcar cards, 44, 46, *49, 50*, 87–89, 206
    television, 145, 148, 150, *151*, 168
    Uneeda Biscuits, 44
    V8 juice, 135
agricultural advice to Campbell's farmers, 110
air drying cabinet, *15*
"Aldrich Family, The", 148
"American" cans, 28
American Chicle Division, 182
American cooking traditions, 69
American food renaissance, 171–81
American Magazine, 89
"Amos 'n' Andy", *120–21*, 124
Anderson, Abraham, *13*, 20, 135, 205
    as founder of Anderson and Campbell, 13
    and Heinz, 26
    and tin cans, 17
    as tinsmith, 13
Anderson and Campbell, 13
    award at Centennial Exposition of 1876–77, 25
    beefsteak tomatoes, *19*

partnership dissolved, 25
    product line, 24
    recipe for chicken soup, 24–25
Anderson Preserve Company, 25–26
anniversary in 1994 of 125 years, 200, 204
Appert, Nicholas, *Book for All Households*, 18
aquarium in Camden, Campbell Soup Company, *201*
Archestratus, 156–57
Armstrong, F. Wallace, 89
Arnott's Biscuits, *180*, 181, 200, 209
"Ash and Trash Survey", 89–90
Associated Sunday Magazines, The, 47
Atwater, Wilbur O., 34
auction, tomato, *66–67*
Audubon, John James, 10
Australia, Arnott's Biscuits, *180*, 181
    birthplace of Johnson, 182
    purchase of Kia Ora Company, 161
Ayer, N. W., 44
baby foods, 136, *138*
bakery products, 154–61, 163
Baltimore turtle soup, 64–65
Bar Harbor, Maine, 117
Bartram, John, 61
BBDO (ad agency), 147, 168
Bean with Bacon Treat, 143
Beard, James, 65, 101
Beecher, Catherine, 16, 21, 90
Beecher, Harriet, 16, 21
Beef Broth
    advertisement, *178*
    and Sauce Lyonnaise, 8
Beef Broth Printanier, 175
Beefsteak Ketchup as product of
    Joseph Campbell & Company, 26–27
beefsteak tomatoes. *See* tomatoes, beefsteak
Belgium, 161
Bellevue-Stratford Hotel, 117
Belote, Julianne, *The Complete American Housewife*, 64
Biardot, Alphonse, 100, 103
Biardot, Ernest, 100
Biardot, Octave, 100
"black broth" of Spartan soldiers, 58
"Bobby Blake and Dolly Drake", 47
boiling temperature, 28
Bonaparte, Napoleon, 18
Bon Appetit, 172
Book for All Households (Appert), 18
booklets for advertising *46*, 53
Borden, Gail, 23–24, 32
Boston Cooking School Cookbook (Farmer), 73
bouillon products, 34
Boulanger, 61
Bounty label, 163, 168
Bourke-White, Margaret, 92, 93, 143
boxes, cardboard, 35, *35*
brand names, 44

brand names, prestige and loyalty, 47
Brans, Jo, 140, 154
bread, 155–57, *160*
breathers, 28
Briar Cliff, 117
bridge tallies, 50
Brillat-Savarin, Jean Antheleme, *The Physiology of Taste*, 32–33
bucket, wooden, *29*
Burnett, Leo, 147–48
"Burns and Allen Show, The", 124
butchers at Campbell plant, *75*
buttons, lapel, 50
Cafe de Paris, 37
Cake, Tomato Soup, 125
calcium chloride, 28
caloric daily requirements, 34
Camden & Amboy "Pea Line", 16
Camden Democrat, 29
Campbell, Carolyn, *Easy Ways to Good Meals*, 139
Campbell, Joseph, *18*, 20, 163, 205, 206
    as partner to Anderson, 21
    recipe for plum pudding, *22*
Campbell, Joseph S., as partner to Joseph Campbell, 26
Campbell Kids, 47–53, 147–48, 206
    advertising *62, 70, 71, 90*
    de-emphasizing, 121–22
    dolls, *48,* 50, *52, 53, 68, 69, 148*
    fiftieth anniversary, 148, *149*
    introduction in 1904, 9
    on postcards, 50, *64, 65*
    products, 148
Campbell Museum, 167–68, 209
Campbell plant workers, *143*
    with can-filling machine, *97*
    filling cans in early version of assembly line, *61*
    loading cooker, *98–99*
    preparing chickens, *93, 145*
    slicing cheese, *96*
    sorting tomatoes, *108–09*
    stirring by hand, *98,* 146
    washing hands, *92*
Campbell products, advertisements, *135, 136.*
    See also specific products
Campbells Menu Book, 121
    contents, 75–80
    introduction, 75
    pages and cover, *74*
    purpose and organization, 80
"Campbell Sound Stage, The", 148
Campbell Soup Company
    acquisition philosophy, 154
    anniversary of 125 years in 1994, 200, 204
    aquarium in Camden, *201*
    baby foods, 136, *138*
    business strategy, 184
    can manufacturing, 135
    chronology, 205–09
    community outreach programs, *202, 203, 204*
    competition, 119
    Delacre purchase, 161, *162*
    Dorrance (Arthur C.) advertising policy, 121–22

Dorrance (Arthur C.) death of, 128
Dorrance (Arthur C.) presidency, 119, 121
Dorrance (John, Jr.) as chairman of the board, 171
    expansion and contraction, 163
    Godiva Chocolatier purchase, 161, *163*
    growth and profits, 117
    home economics department, 139
    international markets, 181–84, *182–83*, 203–04, 208–09
    Johnson as eighth president, 181–82
    Kia Ora purchase, 161
    licensed collectible products, *184, 185*
    McGovern as president, 171
    McGowan as successor to Arthur C. Dorrance, 130
    McGowan's retirement as president, 137–38
    military workers, *129, 130–31*
    Murphy as president, 138
    Murphy's end of presidency 169, 171
    mushroom growing business, 132
    newly formed company, 104, 207
    North American Division, 182
    offices, 136–37
    Pepperidge Farm purchase, 160–61
    plant No. 2 in Camden, 113
    principles of operation, 137
    privately owned to publicly offered stock, 138, 208
    product line changes, 124, 128, 130, 138, 163
    purchase of V8 juice, 132, 134
    in restaurant business, 171
    sales figures, 136, 163, 184, 208, 209
    Shaub as president, 171
    statistics, 200, 203
    Swanson purchase, 152, 154
    test kitchens, *141*
    top-ten selling soups of 1992, 185–87
    and war effort, 128, *129,* 130
    workers. *See* Campbell plant workers
Campbell Soup Fund, 208
Campbell's Soup Farms, 109, 110
"Campbell's Soup position", 89
Campbell's Tomato Soup recipe booklet cover, *77*
Campbell's Treasury of Recipes, 139
Campbelltown, "industrial utopia", *81*
candy business, 161
canneries, early products of, 13
canning
    See also food preservation
    Appert as "father of canning", 19
    Appert's process of, 18–19
    and boiling temperature, 28
    and commercial pressure-cooking kettle, 28
    early history of, 17–29
cans, tin. *See* tin cans
C. A. Swanson & Sons, 152–54
ceramic mincemeat bowl, *26*
chain grocery stores, 86
Chalmers, Irena, 184
Chaplin, Charlie, *41*

Chaptal, Jean Antoine, 33, 34
Chesapeake Bay diamondback terrapins for soup, 65
Chicken Divan, 8, 140
Chicken in Mushroom and Wine Sauce, 140
Chicken Noodle Soup
    and "Amos 'n' Andy", 124
    introduced, 207
    and Nathalie Dupree, 7
Child, Julia, 101
China, 182
chronology, Campbell Soup Company, 205–09
Chunky Soups, *168,* 169, 171, 209
Cimino, Michael, 168
Cinnaminson, New Jersey,
    Dorrance home and farm, *33,* 84, *87,* 109, 117
city markets, *66*
Civil War, and canning industry, 23
Claiborne, Craig, 101
clam chowder, 61
Cobbett, William, 15
cold soups, 151
Colket, Charlotte, *116*
Colket, Ethel Dorrance, *116*
Colket, Tristrain C., Jr., *116*
collectible products, *184, 185*
Commercial Canning in New Jersey, 27
community outreach programs, Campbell Soup Company,
    202, 203, 204
Complete American Housewife, The (Belote), 64
concentrated soup stocks, 34, 54, 70, 125
condensed milk, 23–24
condensed soups
    early production, *44–45*
    first five varieties, 37
    and John Dorrance, 9, 32–37
Consomme advertisement, *122*
consumers
    advertising directed at, 145, 147
    all classes, 90
Continental Can Company, 135
Continental cooking traditions, 7, 13, 32, 65, 69, 70
conveyer line in Camden factory, *113*
cookbooks, *63,* 75, 101, 127, 172
    See also specific titles
    gourmet, *172, 173,* 172–75
    soup, 139, 147, *175*
    written by Campbell home economists, 139
cooking schools, 73, 172
cooking shows on television, 101, 172
Cooking with Condensed Soup, 139, *147*
cooking with soup, 207. *See also* sauces, gravies
Cooper, Jacob, 10
Cooper, James Fenimore, 18
Cordon Bleu Cooking School (London), 7
corn-and-chicken soup of Pennsylvania Dutch, 65
Cornell University football team uniforms, 37, 46, 206
Cortes, Hernando, 106
Cream of Broccoli Soup, *186,* 187
Cream of Mushroom Soup, *111, 171*
    gravy recipe, 127
    and green bean casserole with onion rings, 7
    and sherry in Chicken Divan, 8
    significance of, 124–25

cream soup, 70
Creative Cook, The, 173
Crescent (company label), *20*
Crine, R. Vincent, 112
Cronin, Betty, 153–54
Cuisine Minceur (Guerard), 178
Culinary Chemistry, 32
Curtis Publishing Company, 89
"Cyclone" machines, 114
De Gouy, Louis P., 144
Delacre purchase by Campbell Soup Company,
    161, *162*, 200, 208
De Lisle, Charles Louis, *69*
Depression, 119, 122
DeVos Lemmens, 200
diamondback terrapins for soup, 65
Directions for Cookery (Leslie), 24, 34, 38
dolls, Campbell Kid, *48*, 50, *52*, *53*, *68*, *69*, *148*
"Donna Reed Show, The", *151*
Donner Party cannibalism, 23
Dorrance, Arthur, 29, 130, 163, 205, 206
    as partner to Joseph Campbell, 26
    as successor to Joseph Campbell, 13
Dorrance, Arthur C., *117*, 207, 208
    death of, 128, 130
    as president of Campbell Soup Company, 119, 121
    younger brother of John, 103
Dorrance, Bennett, 209, *116*
Dorrance, Charlotte, *116*
Dorrance, Elinor, *116*
Dorrance, Ethel, *116*
Dorrance, Ethel Malinckrodt
    (Mrs. John T. Dorrance), 84, 103, *116*
Dorrance, George Morris, older brother of John, 103
Dorrance, John T., *32*, 152, 163, 203–04, 206, 207
    ahead of his time, 177
    chef training, 37–38, 70
    and condensed soups, 9, 32–37
    and Continental cuisine, 7, 13, 32, 65, 70, 72
    death of 117, 119
    education of, 13, 30
    family tree, *116*
    as head of company, 84–86, 117
    hiring by Joseph Campbell Preserve Company, 30, 206
    home in Cinnaminson, New Jersey, *33*, 84, *87*
    laboratory in Camden, *33*
    and love of soup, 84, 98
    as marketing genius, 9, 30, 38–42
    marriage and family, 84, 117
    promotions in company, 42, 44, 55, 56
    as schooner hand, 17
    and soup image, 167
Dorrance, John, III, *116*
Dorrance, John, Jr., *116*, *171*
    and Campbell Museum, 167–68
    chairman of the board of Campbell Soup Company, 171
Dorrance, Margaret, *116*
Dorrance, Mary Alice, *116*
Draps, Josef, 161
Drayton, Grace Gebbie, *47*, *49*, 50
drying foods, 15, 17
dry soup mix
    with Campbell label, 167
    with Franco–American label, *127*, 128

Dupree, Nathalie
    and Chicken Noodle Soup, 7
    forward by, 6–9
    making up recipes, 7, 8
Durand, Peter, 20
Durkee, 209
Eastman, George, 30
Easy Ways to Good Meals (Marshall and Campbell), 139
Edison, Thomas, 30
eggs, preservation of, 18
E. I. Horsman Company, 50, 148
Entenmann's, Inc., 182
Enterprise machines, 93, 97
Epictetus, 200
Eresus, 157
Escoffier, Auguste, 9, 65, 125, 144
Escoffier, Auguste
    Guide to the Fine Art of French Cuisine, A, 35, 65
    on history of soup, 58
    on value of soup course, 72
    and rich stocks, 70
European Common Market, 182
European market, *82*, *83*
Everybody's Magazine, 44
exotic soups advertisement, *123*
experimental farm, 87
factory conveyer line at Camden, *113*
family tree, John Dorrance, *116*
fan as promotion item, *109*
farm, experimental, 87
Farmer, Fannie Merritt, 37, 70, 90
    Boston Cooking School Cookbook, 73
farms, Campbell's Soup Farms, 109, 110
Fennel, Paul, 147
Fisher, M. F. K., 101
    How to Cook a Wolf, 143–44
food, early distribution and storage of, 14–15
food preparation
    at the Campbell factory, *60*
    at home, *61*
food preservation
    See also canning
    air drying cabinet, *15*
    before Civil War, 15
    containers for, 18, 20–21
    drying, 15, 17
    early history of canning, 17–29
    freezing, 17, 151–54
    microbiology of, 17
    pickling, 15–16
    pressure cooker, *17*
    rack for canning jars, *16*
    and refrigeration, 17
    salting, 17–18
food renaissance in America, 171–81
Ford, Henry, 30
formal dinners, 80–82
Fortnum and Masons, 7

Fortune (magazine), 92, 143
FR-8, 151, *153*
Frailey, Leonard, 44, 121
Franco-American, 38, 41, 135–36, 163, 200
    booklet cover, *102*
    cream sauce, *103*
    dry soup mix, *127*, 128
    as first canned soup producer, 13, 32
    gold medal, *100*
    gravies, 136
    history of, 100–103
    information booklet, *86*
    kitchens, *101*
    labels of food products, *104*
    Macaroni, 128
    Macaroni and Cheese, 136
    products of, 101
    purchase by John T. Dorrance, 103–04, 207
    reinvigoration of, 136
    Spaghetti a la Milanaise, 104, 135
    spaghetti measurement, *94–95*
    Spaghetti O's, 177, 208
Fray Bentos, 200, 209
freezers, home, 152
French cuisine. *See* Continental cooking traditions
frozen food, 151–54
frozen soups, 151–52, *154*, *155*
fruit juices, 151, *153*
fruit soups, 151, *152*
Fussel, Betty, 101, 125
F. Wallace Armstrong, 89
garlic, 125, 174
garnish, soup, 54
Gazos Creek, CA, 132
gelatinous soup, 70
General Foods, 136
general stores, 86
Gerber Products, 182
glass bottles for canning, 18, 20–21
Glasse, Hannah, 70
global marketplace. *See* international markets
Godiva Chocolatier, 161, *163*, 200, 208
Godsen, Freeman, 124
golden apples, *pomi d'oro*, 106
Golden Mushroom Soup, *171*
gold medals, 41, *100*, 206
Good Housekeeping,
    Campbell's first magazine advertisement, 206
    Magazine Bureau of Food and Sanitation and Health, 90
Gorton-Pew Fisheries, 103
gourmet cookbooks, *172*, *173*, 172–75.
    See also international cuisine
Graham, Sylvester, 157
gravies, *171*
    Franco-American, 136
    recipes, *63*, 125, 127
Great Depression, 119, 122
Green Bean Bake, 7, 140–41, 145
grocery business, 86–87
grocery stores,
    turn-of-the-century, *25*, 36–37

window layouts, *51*
Guerard, Michel, *Cuisine Minceur*, 178
Guide to the Fine Art of French Cuisine, A (Escoffier), 35, 65
Gunn Richards and Company, 55
Hall, Harry, Superintendent of Campbell's
    Soup Farms, 109, 112
hammer mill, 114
hand labor, 93, *98, 143, 146*
Hanover Trail Steak House, 171
Harrison, Mrs., *Housekeeper Pocketbook*, 27
Harrods, 7
Healthy Request, 181
Heiferling, Mindy, 178
Heinz, 119
Heinz, H. J., 26
Helps for the Hostess, 90, 121, 175, 207
    contents, 80–82
    cover of, *79*
    pages from, *78*
    purpose and organization, 80
    sauce recipe, 125
"Henry Morgan's Great Talent Hunt", 148
Henry, Patrick, 70
Hill, Dorrance, *116*
Hill, Hope Happy, *116*
hole and cap, 21
Hollingshead chemical plant, 10
"Hollywood Hotel", 124
home economics department, Campbell Soup Company, 139
home freezers, 152
homemade soup vs Campbell's soup, 6, 66, 69, 90, 167
Hormel, 119
horse drawn delivery trucks, *54*
Horsman, E. I., 50, 148
Hotel McAlpin, 103
Housekeeper Pocketbook (Mrs. Harrison), 27
House of Appert, The, 19
housewife, American, 73, 90, *125*
Houston, Bruce, 187
"Howdy Doody Show, The", 148
How to Cook a Wolf (Fisher), 143–44
Huckins (company), as first canned soup producer, 13, 32, 38
Hungry-Man Dinners, Swanson, 169, *170,* 171
Hurrell-Disney Studios, 147
ice and early refrigeration, 17
icebox, 17. *See also* refrigeration
ice cream, 17
Indian foods
    pork and beans, 54–55, *56, 57*
    soups, 61–64
    succotash, 22
industrial parks, Campbelltown, *81*
International Cook, The, 173
international cuisine, 171–72, *176,* 177.
    See also gourmet cookbooks
international markets, 181–84, *182, 183,* 203–04, 208, 209
Iriquois tribe, 61–64

"Iron Chink", 27
jams, 15
Japan, 182, 209
Jefferson, Thomas,
    and French cuisine, 70
    and tomatoes, 106, 109
jellied consomme, 151
jellied portable soup, 34
jellies, 15
jingles, 49–50, 97, 150, 168
Johnson, David W., 181–82, 203–04, 209
Johnson, Dr. Samuel, 61
Johnson, Robert Gibbon, 109
Johnston and Cushing Studios, 147
Joseph Campbell & Company, 26, 28–29
Joseph Campbell Company
    delivery trucks, *55*
    downsizing product line, 54
    factory in 1912, *54*
    growth of, 82
    introduction of pork and beans, 54–55
    move from Camden to Gloucester County, 55–57
    name change to Campbell Soup Company, 104, 207
    name change to Joseph Campbell Company, 53
    purchase by John Dorrance, 55, 57
    twenty-one varieties soup product line, 65–72
Joseph Campbell Preserve Company
    advertising at turn-of-the-century, 44
    article of incorporation, 29
    Camden office and factory, *13*
    first annual report, *12*
    foundation and growth of, 13
    and John Dorrance, 29
    location of, 10, 13
    name change, 53
    products of, 29
JTD tomato, named for John Thompson Dorrance, 112
Juice Works, 181
Kennett Square, PA, 132
Kerrigan, Nancy, 9
ketchup, 23, 24, 26, 27, *163*
Ketterlineus Lithographic Manufacturing Company, 47
kettles,
    nickel, *97,* 114
    production line, *80*
Kia Ora purchase by Campbell Soup Company, 161
kitchens
    at Franco-American, *101*
    test, *146*
    turn-of-the-century, *34*
Knowles, William G., 25
Kodak camera, 47
labels
    of Joseph Campbell and Company, *20, 21*
    of Joseph Campbell Preserve Company, *28*

for ketchups, 23
for mincemeat, 27
original color and design for soup label, *27, 37*
origin of red and white, 37, 46
private, 20, 23
Labels for Education, 202, 209
Ladies Home Journal, 89, 90
Lamb, Charles, 58
"Law Sakes Alive! What are You Doing Baby?" (Markham), 16
Lane, Frankie, 168
lap-eating, 154
lapel buttons, 50
"Lassie", 148–50, *151*
leathers, 15
Lee, General Robert E., 23
Le Menu frozen dinners, 178
Leo Burnett, 147–48
Lesbos, 156–57
Leslie, Eliza, *Directions for Cookery*, 18, 24, 34, 38
licensed collectible products, *184, 185*
Life (magazine), 92, 148
Lincoln, Abraham, 16, 64
"Little Joker", 28
locker plants, 152
Louden Packing Company, 134
Louisiana cuisine, 69
Louis Stern Gallery, 187
Louis XV, 61
low fat products, 181
low sodium products, 181
Macaroni, Franco-American, 128
Macaroni and Cheese, Franco-American, 136
McGovern, R. Gordon, 171, 181–82, 203, 209
McGowan, James, 130, 137–38, 208
machine labor, adding noodles to cans, 144
McLean, Mrs. Edward B., 117
magazine, 50, 53, 206
maids as food servers, 81–82
Main Line Philadelphia, 84, 117
Malinckrodt, Ethel (Mrs. John Dorrance), 84, 103, 116
Manhandlers, 168, 169
Manning, James, 29
Margaret Rudkin Pepperidge Farm Cookbook, The (Rudkin), 160
Marie's Cafe, 208
Marie's Salad Dressings, 181, 200, 208, 209
marketing
    See also advertising
    "Ash and Trash Survey", 89–90
    by John Dorrance, 38–42
    genius of Campbell's, 9
    Kerrigan in 1994, 9
    price is right, 41, 53, 98
    research, 89–90
    salesmen, 87, 88–89
markets, city, 66
Markham, Charles, 16
Marshall, Ann, Easy Ways to Good Meals, 139

Martineau, Harriet, 15
meal planning and recipes. *See* menu books
meat-and-potatoes era, 139, 145
medals, gold, 41, 100, 206
menu books,
    Campbell's Menu Book pages and cover, 74, 75
    Rorer's entire year's meals, 73
"Mickey Mouse Club, The", 148
microbiology of food preservation, 17
Middle Ages soup, 58
military workers at Campbell Soup Company, 129, 130–31
milk, condensed, 23–24
"milk sick, the", 16
mincemeat, 27
Miniature Quiches, 173–74
Missentop, 117
"M'm! M'm! Good!", 7, 9, 150, 182
mom-and-pop corner stores, 86
Montana, 117
Montgomery Ward, 148
Morgenthau, Henry, 117
Morrison, Samuel Eliot, 16
Mrs. Paul's Kitchens, 200, 208, 209
Mulligatawny Soup, 177
Murphy, William B., 127–28, 130, 208, 209
    and Campbell Museum, 167–68
    end of presidency, 169, 171
    and mushroom-growing business, 132
    as president of Campbell Soup Company, 138
    product development, 132
    in test kitchen, 141
    and tomato juice, 132
    and Warhol, 164
Mushroom Almond Sauce, 143
mushroom-growing business, 132
mushroom soup. *See* Cream of Mushroom Soup
Nakano Vinegar, 209
National Biscuit Company, 44
Needham, Louis & Brorby, 147
New Jersey Agriculture Station, 112
New Jersey produce, 22
newspaper, 50, 53
New York Shipbuilding yards, 10, 13
New York Times, 84, 172
New York Tribune, 90
nickel kettles, 97, 114
Nielsen Food Index, 128
non-profit corporation, Campbell Soup Fund, 208
North American Division, Campbell Soup Company, 182
"nouvelle cuisine", 178, 181
"Nouvelle Hell", menu, 178
Noyes, Arthur, 30
nutrition, 34–35
N. W. Ayer & Son, 44
offices of Campbell Soup Company, 136–37
Ogilvy, Benson, and Mather, 147
okra, 69
Onion Soup, advertisement, 140
Open Pit Barbeque Sauce, 181, 209
Paillards, 37, 38

Panic of 1896, 29
Paris Exhibition of 1900, gold medal for Campbell, 41, 206
Parlin, Charles Coolidge, 89
Paul Fennel Agency, 147
Pauli, Corinne, 147
Peacock, W. G., 134
Peanut Butter Bisque, 143
Pennsylvania Dutch corn-and-chicken soup, 65
Pepperidge Farm, 154–61, 163, 200
    See also Rudkin, Margaret
    advertisements, *159*
    founding of, 207
    Margaret Rudkin, *158*
    mechanized cookie making, *161*
    purchase by Campbell Soup Company, 160–61, 208
    recipe for bread, *160*
Percheron horse drawn delivery trucks, *54*
Perfect Tuna Casserole, 140, 145
Philadelphia Press and Evening Journal, 47
Philadelphia turtle soup, 65
Phillips, Albanus, 119
Phillips Food Company, 119
Physiology of Taste, The (Brillat-Savarin), 32–33
pickling foods, 15–16
Pierce, Anne Lewis, 90–93
Pietro's Pizza, 171
place cards, 50
Plant No. 2 in Camden, 113
plumb joint, 21
plum pudding, recipe for, *22*
Polish Soup, 144
pomi d'oro, golden apples, 106
pork and beans, 54–55, *56, 57*, 104, 206
postcards, souvenir, 50, *64, 65*
potato farm, *14–15*
pot liquor, 61
Prego spaghetti sauces, 178, 181, 200, 209
prepared foods as major industry, 9
preservation of food. *See* food preservation
preserve closet, 15
pressure cooker, *17*, 28
prices of products, 41, 53, 98
Prince Crossing, IL, 132
Prince of Wales, 38
principles of operation, Campbell Soup Company, 137
Printanier Soup, 177
Printer's Ink, 122
production line of kettles, *80*
product line
    changes in, 124, 128, 130, 138, 163
    downsizing, 54
    top-ten selling soups of 1992, 185–87
    of twenty-one varieties of soup, 65–72
promotional products, 50, *150, 184, 185*
    See also Campbell Kids, dolls
    ceramic mincemeat bowl, *26*

dresses, *184*
    fans, *109*
protein dailey requirements, 34
Proust, Marcel, 167
quality control of John T. Dorrance, 37–38
quiche, 173–74
Rabelais, Francois, 61
radio, 122, 124
Radnor mansion, 117
Radnor, PA, 84
Randolph, Mary, 73
Reagan, Ronald, 135, *137*
recipes
    See also cookbooks; menu books; specific foods
    with Campbell's soup, 7, 8
    creation of by John T. Dorrance, 34–35
    as trade secrets, 93
red and white labels, 37, 46
refrigeration, early history of, 17
renaissance in American food, 171–81
Renaissance soup, 58
research, market, 89–90
restaurant, origin of word, 61
restaurant business, Campbell Soup Company, 171
retort, 28
Reyniere, Grimod de la, 72
Ritz, 103
Rochambeau, Comte de, 14
Rockwell, Norman, 122
Romans and soup, 58
Root, Waverly, 61
Rorer, Sarah Tyson, 73, 90
Rudkin, Margaret, 154–61, 163, *158*, 207
    The Margaret Rudkin Pepperidge Farm Cookbook, 160
Ryan, Thomas Fortune, 117
Sacramento, CA, 132
sales figures, 136, 163, 184, 208, 209
salesmen, 87, *88–89*
salt pork, 17–18
Sanwa ramen noodle soups, 209
Saturday Evening Post, 89
sauces, 140, 143, *171*
    condensed soups used as, 34, 125
    Lyonnaise, 8
    recipes, 125, 127
Scandinavia, 151
schools, cooking, 73
sculpture, *187*
Sears, 148
"sermon on soup", 98, 100
Shaub, Harold A., 171, 181–82, 203, 209
Simmons, Amelia, 16
Simply Delicious Recipes, 209
Smith, Harold, 208
Smith, Jessie Wilcox, 122
Snyder, Charles, 47
Societe de Secours Mutuels et de Retraite
    des Cuisiniers de Paris, 37–38
solder top, 21
sop, 61

soup
    See also specific kinds
    cold, 151
    combinations of, *63*, 143–44
    cookbooks, 139, 147, *175*
    cooking with, 207. *See also* sauces, gravies
    as first course, 72, 168
    frozen, 151–52, *154*, *155*
    history of, 58–65
    origin of word, 61
    and salad advertisement, *179*
soupe, 61
Souperburgers, 145
Souperman, 182
Soup Indienne, 175
Soup Mates, *63*, 143–44
souvenir postcards, 50, *64*, *65*
Spackman, Walter, 26, 29
spaghetti
    becomes pasta, 177–78
    Franco-American Spaghetti O's, 177
    measurement at Franco-American plant, *94–95*
Spaghetti a la Campbell, 125
Spaghetti a la Milanaise, 104, 135
Spaghetti with Campbell's Tomato Soup, 177
Spallanzani, Lazaro, 18
Spartan soldiers' "black broth", 58
springers, 28
Standard Brands, 132, 134, 136
Star Wars Cookies, 181
stock, soup, 34, 54, 70, 125
Stout Hearted Soups, 168, *169*
Strawbridge, Diana, *116*
Strawbridge, George, Jr., *116*
streetcars, advertising in, 44, 46, *49*, *50*, 206
stud hole, 21
sumptuary laws, 61
Suntory, 182
Swanson, 200, 208, 209
    Hungry-Man Dinners, 169, *170*, 171
    purchase by Campbell Soup Company, 152, 154
Swanson, Carl, 152–54
Swanson, Clarke, 153
Swanson, Gilbert, 153
Sweden, rural, *83*
swells, 28
table setting, 81
tablette de bouillon, 34
"takeouts", 61
television advertising, 145, 148, 150, *151*, 168
television cooking shows, 101
terrapins for soup, 65
tin
    in refrigerators, 13, 17
    as roofing material, 13
    in tin cans, 17
tin cans, manufacture of, 21, 28, 135
tomatoes

    auction of, *66–67*
    beefsteak, 13, *19*
    botanical background, 106
    cultivating and developing, 109, 110, 112–14
    grading, 113–14
    history, 106, 109
    JTD tomato named for John Thompson Dorrance, 112
    processing for soup, 113–14, 116
    and Thomas Jefferson, 106, 109
    trucks of, *107*
    varieties, 112
    workers sorting, *108–09*
Tomato Juice
    as a commodity, 132
    advertisements, *118*
    label, *134*
Tomato Soup
    of the 1890s, 6
    advertisements, *110*, *112*, *178*
    cooking process, 114, 116
    most popular of the twenty-one kinds, 109
    recipes, 125, 177
    and Warhol, 164
top-ten selling soups of 1992,
    Campbell Soup Company, 185–87
trade secrets, recipes, 93
trucks, delivery, *54*
tuna casserole recipe, 140, 145
tureens, soup, *72*, *73*, *166*, *167*, 168
turtle soup, 64–65
TV dinners, 153–54, *156*, *157*, 208
    Swanson Hungry-Man Dinners, 169, *170*, 171
Twain, Mark, 38
twenty-one varieties of soup, 65–72, *89*, *124*, 127–28
Underwood, William, 19–20
Uneeda Biscuits, 44
Union Army, 23
United States Congress bill on nutritive values of foods, 34
V8 juice, *133*, 135
    development of, 134
    in Japan, 182
    purchase of from Standard Brands, 132, 134, 208
vacations of John Dorrance family, 117
Van Sciver, Joseph, 10
Veal Mediterranean, 174
vegetable juices, 134
Vegetable Soup
    of the 1890s, 6
    advertisements, *104*, *115*, *119*, *126*
    cooking directions, 93, 97
vegetarian cookery, *174*
Veg-min, 134
Victor Talking Machine Company, 10
Vlasic, Joseph, 208

Vlasic Pickles, *181*, 200, 208, 209
Voit, Karl von, 34
Waldorf, 37
Ward, Wheelock, 89, 147
Warhol, Andy, 7
    Campbell name as icon, 184
    commission to paint soup box, 209
    first soup can painting, 208
    and love of Campbell's soup, 164, 167
    portfolio of the Campbell Image, 188–199
Warner Lambert, 182
War Production Board, 128
wartime
    advertisements, *127*, *128*
    field rations from Campbell Soup Company, 128, *129*
    military workers at Campbell Soup Company, *129*, *130–31*
Washington, George, food at Mount Vernon, 14
Weiner, Dan, 140, 143, 146
Wheelock, L. Ward, 89, 147
white bread, 157, *160*
Whitney, Payne, 117
whole-wheat bread, 156–57
whole-wheat flour, 156–57
Wiederseim, Grace. *See* Drayton, Grace Gebbie
Wiederseim, Theodore, 47
Wilder, Billy, 187
wine, cooking with, 174
women entering work force, 171
Wonderful Ways with Soups, 139, 143, 144, *147*
Woodcrest, 117
workers at Campbell plant. *See* Campbell plant workers

Photo Credits and Copyrights

All of the photos have been provided courtesy of
Campbell Soup Company Archives, except the following:
The Bettmann Archive, New York: 14–15, 25, 59, 61, 66;
Margaret Bourke-White. 1935. Photos courtesy Syracuse
University Library, Department of Special Collections.
Reproduced courtesy Jonathan and Roger White: p. 85, 92, 93
(above and below), 94–95, 96, 97, 98–99; The New-York
Historical Society, New York: p. 16 (Charles Markham.
"Law Sakes Alive! What are you doing, Baby?". ca. 1872. Oil on
canvas, 44 3/4 x 58 3/4". Courtesy The New-York Historical
Society, New York); Courtesy of Louis Stern Gallery, Beverly
Hills, California: p. 187 (Billy Wilder and Bruce Houston.
Variation on a Theme by Queen Nefertete I. 1993. Sculpture,
8 x 4 x 5 1/2". Photo by Brian Forrest); © 1994 The Andy
Warhol Foundation for the Visual Arts, Inc., New York:
p. 164 (*Campbell's Soup I (Tomato)*. 1968. From a portfolio of
10 screenprints printed on white paper, 35 x 23".); 165 (*100
Campbell's Soup Cans*. 1962. Synthetic polymer paint on canvas,
72 x 52". Albright-Knox Art Gallery, Buffalo, New York. Gift
of Seymour Knox); 188, 189, 190, 191 (all), 192 (all), 194–195,
196, 197 (left and right), 198 (all), 199; Dan Weiner. 1955.
Reproduced courtesy Sandra Weiner: p. 108, 141, 142, 143
(above and below), 144, 145, 146 (above and below).